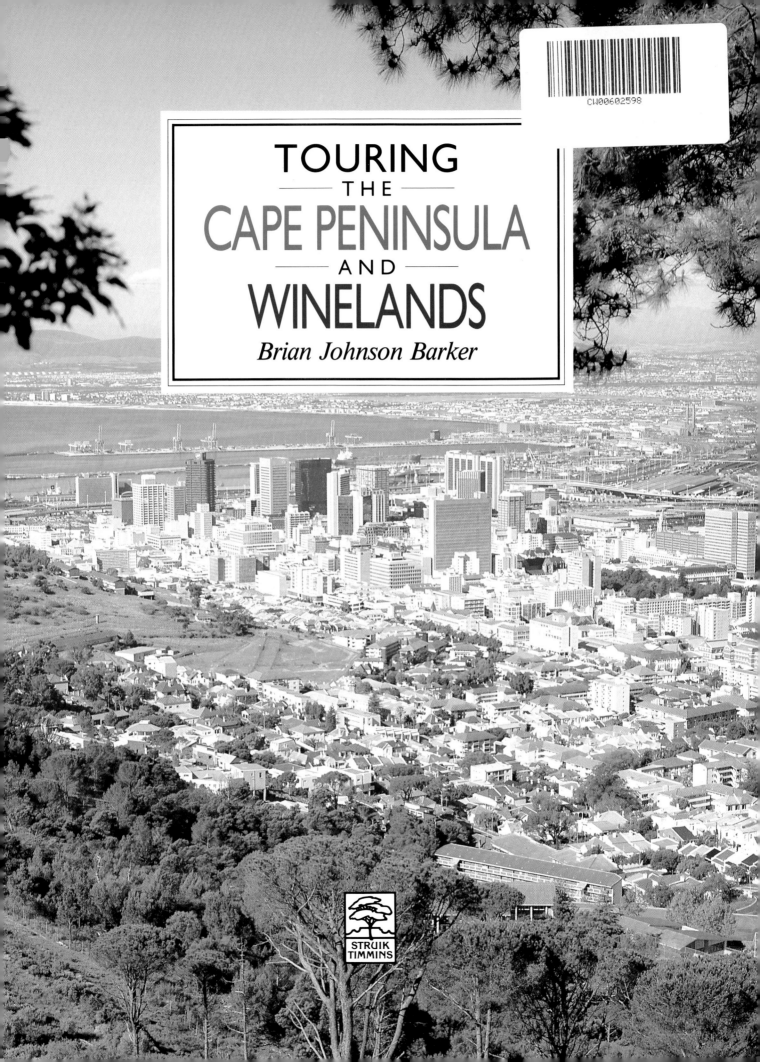

TOURING
THE
CAPE PENINSULA
AND
WINELANDS

Brian Johnson Barker

STRUIK
TIMMINS

Struik Timmins Publishers (Pty) Ltd
(a member of the Struik Group (Pty) Ltd)
Struik House
80 McKenzie Street
Cape Town 8001

Reg. No.: 54/00965/07

First published 1991

PHOTOGRAPHERS
Gerald Cubitt (GC); Roger de la Harpe (RdlH); John Haigh (JH);
Roy Johannesson (RJ); Walter Knirr (WK); Jean McKinnon (JMc); Jean Morris (JM);
Ian Nienaber (IN); Kristo Pienaar (KP); Ethel Rosenstrauch (ER); August Sycholt (AS);
Janek Szymanowski (JS); Mark van Aardt (MvA); Hentie van Jaarsveldt (HvJ)

Cover design by Robert Meas
Typesetting by Struik DTP
Reproduction by Unifoto (Pty) Ltd, Cape Town
Printed and bound by Kyodo Printing Co (Singapore) Pte Ltd

ISBN 0 86978 488 9

CONTENTS

Cape Town City

Cape Town is a unique tapestry of its people, its places and its incomparable setting, all inextricably woven on a cloth of recorded history that is more than three centuries old. This is not where Europe met southern Africa for the first time, but this is where Europe came to stay, and to create here something of itself, a slow, harmonious blend with Africa.

The setting of Cape Town, between the blue of the bay and the distinctive bulk of Table Mountain, is one of the most attractive in the world, and the city that has grown here is worthy of its surroundings. It all started as a vegetable patch, in 1652, when the Dutch settlement was established to grow and supply vegetables and bartered meat to Dutch ships passing on their way to or from the spice-rich East Indies.

The shoreline then was very different, and the seas lapped high up Adderley Street – you can see the old shoreline marked in bronze on the floor of the Golden Acre shopping complex. Here too you can see the old reservoir, from which pioneering seamen drew casks of water to store on their white-sailed ships.

And although the vegetable garden soon became a botanical garden, at least one of the old fruit trees – a pear – still faithfully bears an annual offering of small, wizened fruit. The stern profiteers of the Dutch East India Company would have approved of this gallant survivor.

Walk along oak-shaded Government Avenue, as Capetonians have done for generations, past the Houses of Parliament and the stately facade of Tuynhuys, official Cape residence of the State President. Sit for a while, and trusting squirrels and pigeons will gather at your feet in the hope of receiving nuts or other small scraps. In the tree-lined Gardens you can enjoy the gracious quiet of the Anglican

Right: *Aerial view of Cape Town's city centre* (MvA)

Cathedral Church of St George the Martyr and the South African Library, with the learned and book-lined shelves, all the fascination of the natural history museum and planetarium, and the art collections of the South African National Gallery.

Trees and flowers, monuments and memorials, are just some of the many aspects of Cape Town, lively city of the fairest Cape.

Left: *Table Mountain* (MvA)
Right: *Flower-seller at the Grand Parade* (ER)

Middle: *Jan Smuts' statue in the Gardens* (MvA)
Above: *Lutheran Church, Strand Street* (GC)
Top: *Houses of Parliament, Government Avenue* (JS)

The Castle of Good Hope

The Dutch settlers built themselves a fort of clay on what is now the Grand Parade, and the present Castle dates only from 1666, when four foundation stones were laid. As well as being headquarters of a military command, the Castle houses part of the William Fehr Collection of Art, complemented by gracious, gleaming old furniture, glassware and the delicate porcelain of the East. There is also a museum of militaria, reflecting occupation of the buildings by the forces of Holland, Great Britain and a united South Africa for over three centuries.

Patient archaeological excavation and reconstruction have restored features long forgotten, like the colonnaded bath and the paved courtyard behind the screen wall that developed into the 'Kat', with its gracious balcony and delicate wrought-iron tracery. By contrast, the dread of ancient punishment hangs heavy in the torture chamber and the grim dungeons where some prisoners, optimistic to the last, carved defiant messages in the wood of the massive doors. Although its guns have never fired a shot in anger, the Castle is said to host a number of ghosts ranging from an unloved, 18th-century governor to a mysterious 'grey lady' who rattles about the cold and stony corridors.

Above: *The 'Kat' balcony, the Castle* (MvA)
Below: *The Castle* (AS)

Bo-Kaap

Slavery at the Cape ended in 1838 and, since that historic day in December, the Cape's Muslim community has shown a tendency to live together, here on the slopes of Signal Hill. In the still of early morning the cry of the muezzin echoes among the narrow, cobbled streets, his voice floating from the tall minarets of the mosques as he calls the faithful to prayer. Traditionally, it was this community that supplied the craftsmen who created so much of the beauty of Cape-Dutch architecture, and the men who reaped the rich harvests of the sea. The best way to see the Malay Quarter, in this part of the city known as Bo-Kaap (Upper Cape Town), is on a guided tour (*see* p94).

Above: *Mosque, Longmarket Street* (JS)
Top left: *Minaret* (JM)
Left: *Bo-Kaap museum, Wale Street* (JS)
Below: *Kramat at Signal Hill* (MvA)

Cape Town inhabitants are protected from fire, flood, famine and earthquake by a circle of Muslim tombs, or kramats, in which are buried holy and learned men of long ago. The identity of some of them is no longer known with any certainty, but their good and kindly deeds are still remembered. A Cape Town newspaper recorded, in 1929, how 'at evening, a lonely figure may be seen toiling up the slope towards the kramat nearest the sea. Sometimes it is an old woman whose child lies at death's door in some dim room in the Quarter; sometimes a young girl on the eve of marriage; at other times a young man about to leave on a long journey, or a bearded tradesman ... they all go to offer up prayers and to burn candles for intercession at the tomb of Tuan Said, the descendant of the prophet...'

Cape Town Harbour

Cape Town is a city of the sea. The sea brought her settlers, and trade. All too often, too, the sea brought sorrow, and the floor of the bay is littered with the bones of lost men and ships. Only in 1870, was a safe, enclosed harbour completed. This is the Alfred Basin, named after a son of Queen Victoria, and young Prince Alfred, Duke of Edinburgh, tipped the first load of rocks to commence work on the breakwater, in 1860. The work was continued by convicts, who were housed in the Breakwater Prison in nearby Portswood Road, where the treadmill still stands, at rest and silent now.

Extensions to the Alfred dock were completed in 1905, and, although South Africa has long been a republic, the imperial connection remains in the name of the Victoria Basin. Here tall ships found shelter from the storms, with lean-lined passenger-steamers and small, busy fishing-boats.

Ships still come and go, for Cape Town remains a working seaport, but the old harbour has been given over to a new life. A brewery, restaurants and museums find place among cranes, and old cannons set into the wharf-side to serve as bollards. Here is Victorian architecture, frilled and fussy with lacy ironwork, solid and sedate befitting the premises of important traders, or honest, unpretentious stonework with corners and surrounds picked out in whitewashed plaster.

Above: *Cape Town's harbour by night* (IN)
Below left: *Mitchell's Brewery* (ER)
Below right: *Maritime Museum next to the dry dock* (ER)

There are two modest towers, different in appearance, but both dedicated to time. The Gothic-style clock tower of 1882 also recorded the state of the tide, and once served the port captain as his office. Today, it is maintained by the Ship Society of South Africa and contains a number of interesting exhibits. The other tower is topped with a ball and spike above its weathered, copper roof, and played a vital part in safe navigation from 1894 onwards. Precisely on the hour, an electric signal generated at the Royal Observatory a few kilometres inland caused the ball to drop. At this exact moment, master mariners and their navigators checked the readings of their chronometers, instruments vital in determining longitude. The noon gun still booms out from Signal Hill but, for purposes of navigation, is not an exact enough signal because of the undetermined time it takes for the sound to reach the harbour.

When you have taken a boat-ride or seen it all from a helicopter, walk awhile to savour the smells of a real harbour, and to feel the atmosphere of antiquity so well in tune with the activities of today.

Above: *Victoria and Alfred Hotel* (JM)
Top left: *The tower which played a vital role in navigation from 1894* (IN)
Top right: *The clock tower built in 1882* (JH)

Table Mountain
HISTORY

Although Portuguese navigator Bartolomeu Dias rounded the Cape – by a wide margin – as early as 1488, the first written record of Table Mountain dates only from 1503, when a squadron under Antônio de Saldanha cast anchor in the bay beneath its sheer, rocky walls. It was a navigational error that put the ships here, and to establish just where he was, De Saldanha climbed Table Mountain. The principal topographical features he saw are those you see today: the peninsula tapering away to the south with, south-east, the broad blue sweep of False Bay which, at that time, was still un-named. Northward, the coast of Africa extended to the far horizon, and beyond that to the ancient Pillars of Hercules at the entrance to the Mediterranean Sea. And in the sea below him De Saldanha saw the two flat discs of land that we know as Robben Island and Dassen Island.

He named this place Tábua do Cabo, the Cape of the Table, but for almost 100 years it was known as Aguada de Saldanha – the watering-place of Saldanha. It was the Dutchman, Joris van Spilbergen who, in 1601, named the bay Table Bay, after the flat-topped mountain. The name of Saldanha Bay became attached to a deep inlet 90 kilometres to the north that, ironically, De Saldanha probably never saw – except, perhaps, from the summit of Table Mountain.

The summit is a broad plateau on two levels, where reservoirs were constructed to supply Cape Town with water that was led by the Woodhead and Apostles tunnels to a filtration plant above Kloof Nek. Implements used in the construction of these waterworks, including an old steam locomotive, are carefully preserved in a museum, which can be visited by appointment, on the lower 'back' Table.

The remains of fortified lines can still be traced in old Cape Town and its adjacent suburb of Woodstock (formerly known as Papendorp). These were built at various times during the Dutch occupation that lasted from 1652, with a British interlude between 1795 and 1803, until 1806. It was the British who built the square, stone blockhouses high on the mountain slopes and garrisoned them with soldiers who, if they became bored by inactivity, at least had the consolation of one of the most scenic views in the world.

Above: *Tearoom at the top of Table Mountain* (GC)
Top left: *Table Mountain in the early morning from Rietvlei* (MvA)
Top centre: *Entrance to the Woodhead Tunnel* (IN)
Top right: *Steam locomotive at the museum* (IN)
Middle: *King's blockhouse, Devil's Peak* (IN)
Left: *Aerial view of Table Mountain, Lion's Head and the city* (MvA)

EFFECT ON CITY

When faint, wispy white fringes of cloud gather on the broad brow of Table Mountain during the warm months of summer, Cape-tonians know they are about to be visited by the Cape Doctor. This is the name some forgotten 19th-century humorist gave to the strong south-east and southerly winds that sweep in from the Atlantic Ocean. In 1857, a Cape newspaper complained that 'the protracted absence of the Cape Doctor ... has seriously affected the public health'. Dust and the germs of disease, it was believed, were blown away by the south-easter. It is certainly true, that well over a century later, the wind clears the air of the city's smog and smoke.

It may blow hard, but the south-easter and its attendant wreath of clouds provide an attractive spectacle. As the moisture-laden air is forced to rise by the mountain across its path, it reaches colder heights and condenses to form the typical tablecloth. Above the city it descends again, with light, fleecy fingers reaching for the lower slopes, only to disappear as they reach warmer layers and evaporate.

There is another tale, of an old resident called Van Hunks who enjoyed nothing more than smoking his pipe somewhere up on the mountain where, one day, he met a stranger who demanded a fill of his strong tobacco. The two smoked for days, each determined to outdo the other, and clouds of smoke rolled over the mountain until, at last, the stranger collapsed. It was only when Van Hunks bent to assist him that he saw the horns protruding from the stranger's head. And that is why some Cape Town people say, when the south-easter is blowing, and clouds wreathe their mountain, that Van Hunks and the Devil are puffing at their pipes again.

Top: *The wreath of clouds of the south-easter* (IN)
Right: *Black south-easter over Devil's Peak* (IN)

The mountain has other effects, as you will find if you attempt to listen to your car radio while you follow one of the scenic drives around its base. Turn a corner here, pass beneath a distant buttress there, and although there are no fewer than six relay transmitters on the mountain, the radio signals flicker and fade. The great Table plays tricks with rainfall, too, so that the western flanks receive less than half the amount that descends on suburbs tucked under the eastern face.

Above: *Cold front* (JH)
Below left: *Cable-station at the base of Table Mountain* (IN)
Bottom left: *The cable-car* (IN)
Below right: *Aerial view of the cable-station* (IN)

There was a plan, once, during the Great Age of steam, to build a railway to the top of Table Mountain. Fortunately this idea, with its attendant risk of forest fires, was forgotten and eventually superseded by the funicular, or cableway, opened in 1929. It took people a long time to become reconciled to what they called 'the pimple' of the upper cable-station on the north-western corner of the mountain, but a trip by this effortless, airy transport thrills all who experience it.

The cable car travels at a leisurely speed of some 16 kilometres per hour, and takes from five to seven minutes to travel between the lower station, at an altitude of 366 metres, and the 1 073 metres summit. Weather permitting, the cableway operates every day of the year, between 8.00 a.m. and 10.00 p.m. from December to April, and from 8.30 a.m. to 6.00 p.m. from May to November. There is a quaint tearoom near the upper station, and viewsites from where nothing obstructs the vista that extends for about 150 kilometres in several directions.

FAUNA

The great wall of rock may look sun-baked and bare, but almost every nook or crevice is home to some creature of the mountain. Many are shy and rarely seen although, on a day when warm air rises against the steep cliffs, you may be lucky enough to see a majestic Black Eagle with wings outspread, unmoving and unafraid, effortlessly riding the updraft as it surveys the slopes for its prey. And when it folds its wings and falls like a thunderbolt, the target is most likely to be the common rock-hyrax, also known as the rock-rabbit or dassie. Surrounded by the suburbs of a major city, the drama of nature endlessly unfolds.

The mountain's chacma baboons are shrewd observers of the passing scene and feed in the daytime, retiring to secure positions among the rocks to pass the night. The natural diet of these dog-faced creatures includes roots and fruit, insects and small reptiles, but they have developed a taste for the titbits that unthinking visitors hand out to them. The baboons soon come to expect these tributes, and may put on a very aggressive display when they are with-held. The other native animals of the mountain still regard humans with some reserve.

The dassie, for instance, is unlikely to be caught by surprise, except, of course, by the sudden strike of the Black Eagle. These agile and furry rodents may be seen at a distance sunning themselves among the rocks, and somewhat resemble overgrown guinea-pigs. Relaxed though they may seem, they are wary and alert, and have remarkably good eyesight. They feed during the day on leaves and other tasty vegetable matter, and sleep at night in little family groups in narrow crevices.

Night is the stalking-time for genet, wild cat and the solitary caracal (desert lynx) that is said to be so fast that, if it hunted by day, it could snatch a flying bird out of the air. Black-and-white quills are likely to be the only evidence you will find that porcupines are at home here too. The porcupine, another solitary night-wanderer, is the largest of African rodents, and may be up to 60 centimetres long, with a short tail that it shakes briskly when alarmed, the loose quills making a loud and intimidating clash.

Top: *Black eagle* (IN)
Right: *Deer in the forest near Rhodes' Memorial* (GC)

Several antelope species including wildebeest (a kind of gnu) graze in large enclosures on the lower slopes of Devil's Peak, the mountain that the first settlers knew as Windberg. In the dappled shade of the pine forests near the Rhodes Memorial, fallow deer, not native to South Africa, but happily settled in, graze and delicately accept offerings from wary visitors. Another introduced species is the Himalayan tahr, an agile antelope completely at home on the rocky slopes and precipices. Theirs was an accidental introduction, when a breeding pair escaped from the Groote Schuur Estate in 1937.

It is the profusion of vegetation that attracts an almost equal profusion of bird life – at least 150 species have been recorded – from the flashing colours of the malachite sunbird to the more sombre grey of the rock pigeon with its swelling, melodious notes. Also attracted by the flowers are the butterflies that include the fast-flying Table Mountain Beauty which, appropriately, is responsible for pollination of the red disa orchid.

The mountain is home, too, to many scuttling, crawling creatures of reptile and insect families. Cobra and harmless grass-snake, and even the sluggish puff adder will do their best to avoid you, and bright-eyed lizards will watch your approach before vanishing as though submerging in the solid rock.

Above: *Baboon* (JH)
Below: *Rock dassie* (IN)

Above: *Agama lizard* (IN)
Right: *Cape rock thrush* (IN)
Far right: *Orangebreasted sunbird* (IN)

FLORA

To General J C Smuts, statesman, botanist and philosopher (1870–1950), Table Mountain was 'a cathedral of the sky' where he often came to worship. It was at a gathering at Maclear's Beacon, highest point of the mountain, that he addressed fellow climbers and said:

'To see the Cape flora in its full glory in spring – with all its exquisite variety and colour – is an experience never to be forgotten. And when there is added the song of birds, the hum of insects, and the intoxication of scents, the magic of life is seen and felt in a way which would be difficult to match elsewhere.'

For sheer variety of species, the Cape floral kingdom is impossible to match within a similar area anywhere in the world. One of six such kingdoms proclaimed by international botanists, it covers a strip of coastal country with Cape Town at its centre. The Cape Peninsula alone has some 2 600 species, which is more than the whole of the British Isles contains, and more, also, than in South Australia, which is almost the size of the entire Republic of South Africa. In addition, the Cape flora has been described as 'one of the richest in the world, and is unique, a high percentage being found nowhere else'.

If this kingdom is most richly dressed in spring, it is by no means bare at other times of the year. Winter-flowering yellow daisies (*Euryops* species) brighten slopes and summit while the many blooms of summer are at rest, and among the *fynbos* or 'fine bush' (low-growing evergreen shrubs), there is always some species putting forth its flowers. This group includes the showy, varied proteas, well represented on Table Mountain.

Bright red *Protea cynaroides*, the King Protea, is found here, and has the largest flower head of any protea, sometimes as much as 30 centimetres across. In early autumn you may see *Protea repens*, the sugar-bush, with its yellow flowers like cups laden with nectar. It may also be coloured deep red, but the pale version is more often seen on the mountain.

Top: *King protea* (IN)
Right: *Bush of Cape reed* (IN)

In cool and shady ravines and along river banks you may find stands of the red *Disa uniflora*, a member of the orchid family, and the one known as Pride of Table Mountain. Its large, hooded flowers appear between January and March, and it is the floral emblem of the Western Province. Reed and heath, agapanthus and watsonia, pelargonium and lowly moss and lichen all add their touch of colour and charm to the stately mountain.

When the first European settlers arrived there were patches of forest in some of the ravines, and it is sad to have to relate that these 'civilized' newcomers soon ruined them. With axe and saw they transformed lovely yellowwood and ironwood, stinkwood and beech into flooring, roof timbers, spade handles and even firewood. The silver tree remains, though, at home on Table Mountain, and you will not find *Leucadendron argenteum*, with its metallic-sheened silvery leaves, very far from this corner of the western Cape.

Stone pine, cluster pine and other 'alien' trees of Europe and North America have, sadly, been planted over the years. However, other exotics such as hakeas and acacias are anathema to local conservationists, because they grow at a rapid rate and, having no natural restraints, soon outstrip the natural foliage which is unable to compete. It has been found that the spread of some hakea species can be controlled biologically, by the introduction of seed-destroying insects. However, this method will not destroy existing plants, which must still be removed mechanically.

Table Mountain has been proclaimed as both a national monument and a nature reserve, and restoration of the delicate ecological balance is a continuing operation.

Top: *Moss and lichen* (IN)
Right: *Silver tree* (IN)

VIEW FROM THE TOP

On some misty autumn mornings Cape Town is lost in a sea of swirling fleece, and if you reach the top of the mountain early enough you can experience the grandeur that is not unlike a great ship sailing calmly though a white and silent sea. The tops of taller buildings, further up the slopes, peep out like buoys to mark your channel until the sun, rising clear, slowly dispels the mists. Yet despite the passing likeness to ship and sea, Table Mountain seems a strange place for a sailor to live 'wild' for 14 months.

Joshua Penny was an American sailor who was press-ganged into Britain's Royal Navy and fought at the Battle of Muizenberg in 1796, when the British occupied the Cape for the first time. Weary of the poor food and savage discipline aboard the warship *Sceptre*, Penny managed to fake illness and was taken ashore. Once on land he evaded his escort and chose as his refuge – the mountain. Years later, he wrote a little book describing his adventures, but nobody was entirely sure he was telling the truth.

He wrote of gathering wild honey, making honey beer, of killing antelope with sticks and stones, of making clothes for himself from animal skins, using as a needle a sharpened piece of bone through which he bored an 'eye' with the point of his pocket knife. He claimed to have lived in caves and wrote that 'It was not troublesome to change my quarters; and by often shifting my abode for a new tenement, I acquired by occupation dwellings enough to make my territory called a city. Thus I lived, unannoyed by wild beasts or press-gangs ...' When he finally came down and smuggled himself aboard a Danish ship, it was to hear that the *Sceptre* had sunk during a storm in Table Bay a few days after he had deserted, with great loss of life.

It all seemed something of a tall story until 1858, more than 150 years later when, under deep layers of dassie droppings, owl pellets and dust, many of his poor possessions were discovered in a cave on the mountain. From the great number of fire-scorched animal bones it was obvious he had occupied the cave for a long time. Old clay pipes, tattered

Above: *Sunset at the top of Table Mountain looking towards Kommetjie* (IN)

Right: Lion's Head, Signal Hill and the city (RdlH)

fragments of his seaman's clothes, a belt buckle and buttons, a neckerchief ring and other relics were carefully collected and are in the possession of the Cape Town City Council. They form part of the exhibits of the municipal museum at the Civic Centre.

Of course, the town that Penny looked out upon was very much smaller then, nor did he have any laid-out view sites. Today, you can look down, from just west of the upper cable-station on to the white sands of the Clifton beaches, with the ever-growing suburb of Camps Bay spreading from the beach ever further up the hillsides. Stretching southward are the Twelve Apostles, once the Gewelbergen or 'Gable Mountains' of the Dutch. From behind the tearoom the vista is one of mountain and sea, with Kommetjie lighthouse in view beyond the curve of Hout Bay. If you were to look to your left you would see the other side of the peninsula, with the warmer waters of False Bay lapping the beaches of Muizenberg.

Joshua Penny would find much that is new to fascinate him in the surroundings of his old home. But sunrise and sunset are still the gentle transference of light and colour that they were in his day.

Above right: *The cableway* (IN)
Below: *Look-out point over Camps Bay* (IN)

Green Point and Sea Point

Sam Wallis was a captain who cared for his crew, so when a smallpox epidemic broke out in Cape Town in 1776, he moved his sick sailors from the town and encamped them at a fine, open site that he called Sea Point. Times change, although the name is the same, and Sea Point has the highest density of population on the peninsula.

On your journey to Sea Point you will pass through the suburbs of Mouille Point and Green Point. There's a pathway in Mouille Point, starting near the entrance to the Victoria and Albert docks, ideal for strollers. Pass by the Tudor-style New Somerset Hospital, still called 'New' although it is well over 100 years old – there was already a Somerset Hospital in existence when it opened in the 1860s. Another fascinating place to visit and close to the hospital is Fort Wynyard Museum, reached from Portswood Road, with interesting displays of artillery in the old fort.

Returning to the beachfront in Mouille Point, some way out in the breakers, a lump of old iron rears from the sea. This is the single-cylinder engine of the steamship *Athens*, wrecked here with total loss of life in 1865. Then there's the lighthouse at Green Point, the oldest on the South African coast, dating from 1824. Capetonians habitually call it the Mouille Point lighthouse, although that particular building was demolished in 1908. A couple of blocks in from the coast, where playing fields abut sports stadium, Green Point lives up to its name. It is a place for meeting, and the complex offers a trimpark and a measured kilometre for joggers.

Top: *Sea Point pavilion* (WK)
Right: *The New Somerset Hospital* (JM)

Starting from Green Point and finishing in Sea Point, there's a broad promenade at the edge of the sea where, in winter storms, the white water surges over the railings and slashes across the path. Interrupted only by Sea Point Pavilion and its swimming baths, this is a place where it's pleasant to stroll, jog or just look at the sea. There are little pockets of sand you can reach by steps down from the promenade, and a number of small pools, including Graaff's Pool, where gentlemen may bathe and sunbathe in the nude. Just seaward, off a car park near the end of the promenade, is an interesting geological exposure, so unusual that it has been declared a national monument. Many ages after sedimentary rock had been laid down here, molten igneous rock from within the earth forced its way to the surface to produce this unusual migmatite zone.

Top left: *Green Point lighthouse* (JH)
Top right: *The promenade at Sea Point* (MvA)
Right: *Artillery display at Fort Wynyard Museum* (JM)

Clifton and Bakoven

Clifton, or Clifton-on-Sea as it was known until fairly recently, was at one time more renowned for its rock-fishing than for its bikini'ed bodies soaking up the sun. There are four beaches, each of which has its loyal devotees, separated by great grey granite boulders. Over summer weekends, you may see yachts moored off Fourth Beach, lifting gently in the swell while those aboard study the forms ashore. This is the 'cold' side of the peninsula (*see* Cape Point p36) and the water, even on very hot days, is distinctly chilly.

The cluster of bungalows below Victoria Road arose way back around the turn of the century when, during the summer months, city families erected tents and camped out on the beaches. Gradually, permanent structures were erected but the land on which they stand was leased by the Cape Town City Council and, until 1929, they were not permitted to be occupied during the months of June, July and August. This forced evacuation during the winter months was a measure to prevent the development of what was feared might become a semi-slum in a prime residential area. For early occupiers who lacked their own transport – and very few had private motor cars in those days – the single-decker electric tram was the only way to and from the area.

Picturesque though they are and were, the bungalows were regarded as 'temporary' until a town-planning survey of 1936 acknowledged that they 'produced a pleasing feature peculiar to the locality which the scheme does not contemplate disturbing'. So existing bungalows were pronounced permanent, but the survey opposed 'an increase in the number of these structures which might lead to depreciation of the amenities of the foreshore'. Ironically, the 'amenities' are today the most valuable in the Peninsula, and frequently change hands for millions of rands.

There was a time, though, when it was barely possible to reach them, as in 1802, when the first reference is made to an earlier name for Clifton – 'the place Cobbler's Hole or Schoenmakers Gat'. There was just a narrow footpath from Sea Point but, so far as is known, there never was a shoemaker living in any hole or cave along the way. However, there may be a clue in the diary of Adam Tas (*see* p73) where he writes that 'Jacobus the

Above: *Clifton's beaches* (JS)
Below: *Clifton's beaches* (GC)

Schoenmaker, scum of a cobbler and his cross-grained slut of a wife ...' attacked a woman who was rescued by a 'Mr Bek'. It's interesting that the first grant of land was made to one R Beck, in 1808, at Schoenmakers Gat.

Beck called his 'country place' Meerzicht and, much altered over the years, it survives as Clifton House along Kloof Road leading up to Kloof Nek. This road is an interesting and scenic drive, with a deviation leading to the Round House, now a restaurant but once a shooting box for old Cape governors, and dating from about 1812. The change of name may have something to do with a Mrs Bess Clifton, who ran the Clifton Hotel in Kloof Road late last century.

There's doubt about the origin of Bakoven too, with some supporting the claim that it was named after a rock resembling an old-fashioned Dutch oven. Unfortunately, nobody is quite sure just which rock it is. Others claim there was once a lime-burner's kiln on the site, where now there is a cluster of bungalows with a small, sandy beach and a rock pool.

Top right: *Clifton's beaches* (GC)
Middle right: *Clifton looking towards Lion's Head* (JH)
Middle left: *Clifton looking towards Lion's Head* (JH)
Right: *Bantry Bay* (JM)
Far right: *Clifton's beaches* (JM)

Camps Bay
and Llandudno

The water-rounded granite boulders of Camps Bay contrast sharply with the jagged backdrop of the peaks known as The Twelve Apostles. This is part of the Sunset Coast, the western side of the Cape Peninsula, where palm trees sway over rolling green lawns, and the wide white sands are a beach-goer's delight. Apart from the in-curving sea, there are cooling pools and a paddling pool for toddlers.

Dutch settlers called the mountains the Gewel-bergen, but this name for Gable Mountains didn't appeal to an English governor of 1820, who renamed them The Twelve Apostles. It seems doubtful whether he counted them very carefully, as most authorities give no fewer than 18 major buttresses. Their names, from north to south, have been given as Kloof, Fountain, Porcupine, Jubilee, Barrier, Valken, Kasteel, Postern, Wood, Spring, Slangolie, Corridor, Separation, Victoria, Grove, Llandudno Peak, Llandudno Corner and Hout Bay Corner. Another source gives only 15 names, but includes peaks named for the saints Peter, Paul, John and Luke, and even a Judas Peak. Count them yourself, and take your choice.

The bricked-up entrance to the Woodhead Tunnel (*see* p12) is to be found in Slangolie Ravine, and can be reached by traversing some 540 steps. Reluctant sailor of the Royal Navy, Joshua Penny (*see* p20) had his home in a cave above Fountain Ravine. Above Camps Bay is one of Cape Town's favourite walks – the Pipe Track. This was originally the service path created when the water pipe was laid from the Woodhead Tunnel to the purification plant at Kloof Nek. It makes a fairly level and very scenic walk of just under seven kilometres each way.

Previous page: *The Twelve Apostles at sunset* (MvA)

Top: *Llandudno* (JS)
Middle left: *Camps Bay beach with Lion's Head in the background* (ER)
Right: *Llandudno* (ER)
Far right: *The wreck of* Romelia *off Llandudno* (JS)

Camps Bay takes its name not from any encampment, but from Ernst von Camptz of Mecklenberg who, on a voyage to the east in 1778, was put ashore at the Cape because of serious illness. By the end of the year he had recovered well enough to marry the wealthy widow Wernich, and thereby become master of the farm Ravensteijn. The bay below his farm, in time became known as 'de baay van Von Camptz'.

Two days in July 1977, saw two ships wrecked along this stretch of coast, fortunately without loss of life, when the derelict tankers *Antipolis* and *Romelia* broke loose from the tug that was towing them from Greece to scrap merchants in Taiwan. *Antipolis* came hard ashore at Oudekraal, and has since been cut down to the waterline, but is still visible. *Romelia* fetched up against Sunset Rocks off Llandudno and broke her back the next day. Only the stern section remains wedged in the grasp of the unyielding granite. Until the sea sweeps it away it will remain, naked and exposed, rather appropriately close to the footpath you follow to Sandy Bay, traditionally the nudists' beach.

Top: *Sunset at Oudekraal* (GC)
Middle: *Camps Bay and the Twelve Apostles* (ER)
Bottom: *The palm trees, lawns and white sands of Camps Bay* (MvA)

Hout Bay

A bronze leopard sits on a rock in the little inlet of Flora Bay and watches the fishing boats as they come and go. Hout Bay is a working harbour, but one with a kindly heart for visitors. On the other side of the bay, there are a number of shops clustered around the harbour where you can buy your food fresh from the sea and eat it on the quayside, or you can dine in some style. One of your choices is the Bressay Bank, a trawler built in Gdansk in 1960, but now, moored in Hout Bay harbour, serving as an unusual restaurant.

Another harbour 'pensioner' is a ship retired from the South African Navy, the SAS *Pretoria*, where you can examine the intricacies of ocean-going warfare. Deep-sea fishing trips are something else that can be arranged, and regular schedules offer romantic daytime and sundowner cruises, as well as one-hour cruises to Duiker Island with its entertaining colony of seals.

Ashore, aside from the World of Birds (*see* p64), don't miss the timeless beauty and symmetry of Kronendal, a Cape Dutch homestead that dates from around 1800, and a fascinating museum of local history, that includes the saga of manganese mining in the mountains above the bay.

The first Dutch settlers at the Cape soon chopped their way through all the trees that grew nearby, and searched further afield for new timber. They found it around this bay, which they then named Hout Bay, and there are still small stands of the indigenous forests to be found on high slopes. The bay received the earliest English place-name in South Africa long before that, when it was known as Chapman's Chaunce, after a British naval officer who rowed into it to investigate the possibility of it offering a safe anchorage.

Top: *Hout Bay harbour* (WK)
Right: *Hout Bay beach* (ER)

Top right: *Flora Bay and the Sentinel* (JM)
Middle right: *SAS* Pretoria *and the* Bressay Bank (JM)
Right: *Craft market on the wharf* (ER)

The old seadog's name has been transferred to Chapman's Peak, now girdled by one of the most spectacular, scenic ocean-view drives in the world. You should travel it in both directions to appreciate it fully. It is an easy drive, with strong retaining walls, and a few places where you can stop to study the view and take photographs. The road, built at the level where the mountain's granite base is overlain by softer shale and sandstone, passes the barracks of East Fort, built by the British in 1795. Below Chapman's Peak Drive, and immediately opposite the barracks is the fortress itself, with ancient muzzle-loading cannons still pointing ominously out to sea. South-bound, you turn a bend to see below you the long white expanse of beach at Noordhoek with the distant Slangkop light-house a pencil-thin tower in the distance. A dark and distant blob on the beach is all that is left of the brand-new steamer *Kakapo*, that went hard ashore in 1900. North-bound, the embrace of Hout Bay and its towering Sentinel is a scene of startling beauty.

The people of Hout Bay, so aware of the beauty of their home surroundings and so eager to protect them, declared themselves informally to be citizens of the Republic of Hout Bay, and there's a tale that one of them was admitted to Egypt by showing his republican (Hout Bay) passport.

Top: *Kronendal* (JS)
Right: *Chapman's Peak Drive* (WK)

Above: *Fishing trawler, Hout Bay harbour* (JM)
Below left: *The fortress' cannons with the Sentinel in the background* (JM)
Below right: *Hobie-cats at Hout Bay's beach* (JM)

Kommetjie
and Scarborough

Kommetjie is named for the saucer-like depression in the rocks, filled by high tides. Lesser pools are fun to explore, to watch the minute forms of life that skip and dart and crawl about their circumscribed, watery world. There is a backwash that makes bathing risky, but it's a great place for surfing.

Sea mists hang lightly in the air above Middle Beach, so the cluster of houses on the steep hillside has become known as Misty Cliffs. The lighthouse at Slangkop was erected in 1914, after mists and miscalculations sent the steamship *Clan Monroe* ashore there several years earlier. Cases of whisky washed ashore, to be gleefully collected by the locals, but the civil authorities were more worried about the main cargo of dynamite and guncotton. (By an odd coincidence, a sister ship, *Clan Stuart*, went ashore on the other side of the peninsula – see p45)

The little beach here changes size and shape with the tides and, in winter, sometimes disappears completely. The many natural pools along this rocky coast invite investigation of their busy life, and the presence of a crayfish-processing factory a short distance to the south at Witsand tells of underwater life in deeper waters. It's interesting to watch the small boats launching and landing in the sandy little bay.

A safe place to swim is the wide estuary of the Schuster's River that you reach by passing through the little village of Scarborough and turning at the feature known as Camel Rock. This natural sandstone formation by the roadside could scarcely have been given any other name, and is seen at its best when approached from the south, or Simon's Town.

Right: *Scarborough* (JM)

Above: *Slangkop lighthouse* (JH)
Below: *Cormorants at Kommetjie* (ER)

Cape Point
PLACES OF INTEREST

'The fairest cape we saw in the whole circumference of the earth' was recorded in the ship's log of the *Golden Hind* in 1580. Sir Francis Drake, having sailed around most of the world, and on his way home to England, was in a position to judge.

Much of the southern end of the Cape Peninsula, thrusting out from the mainland, like the prow of a ship, rises almost sheer from the sea, and safe landing-places are few. But somewhere along this coast, historians believe, Bartolomeu Dias, in 1488, planted the stone pillar or padrão dedicated to São Felipe. Others claim that he erected it in Table Bay, but what is certain is that no trace of it has ever been found. Dias Beach, most southerly of the peninsula beaches, is popularly believed to have been the chosen site. Here, in 1975, a floating crane that had broken loose from its towing vessel was washed ashore and soon smashed by the sea.

The beach at Olifantsbosch is a lonely place of dune, sand and rocks, and of great hulks of rusting metal that once formed the hull of the steamship *Thomas T Tucker*. While on her maiden voyage and dodging a real or imaginary submarine in 1942, the ship, loaded with war supplies, struck Albatross Rock some distance offshore, and was beached here in a sinking condition. Fortunately, the valuable supplies were removed before the seas tore the ship to the twisted fragments that remain today. Under the sands here lie the wooden remains of another sad ship, *La Rozette*, of France. In 1786 her crew mutinied, killed the officers and ran her ashore at this isolated spot. Spending money too freely in Cape Town some days later, the mutineers were confronted with their crime and eventually executed.

Some little way to the north of Olifantsbosch the maps show a place marked as Italiaanse Kerkhof – Italian Churchyard. Here were buried the crew of the barque *Caterina Doge*, wrecked nearby in 1886, while carrying a cargo of coal from Cardiff to Cape Town. By a strange coincidence, another Italian ship on the same run, *Carlotta B*, was also wrecked here just two months later.

Above: *Da Gama beacon* (JH)

Right: *The floating crane which was washed up on Dias Beach* (MvA)
Middle: *Cape Point* (MvA)

The Dias monument, a stylized replica of a Portuguese padrão, overlooks the picnic sites and sparkling white beach of Platboombaai, across the peninsula from Olifantsbosch, on the False Bay side. Little tidal pools hold interesting communities of varied creatures like starfish and sea anemones. Another beach popular with picnickers is Bordjierif, site of a second replica padrão, this one to the memory of Vasco da Gama, who was the first man known to have sailed from Europe to India, where he cast anchor in 1498.

In the early morning, the sandstone ledges of Rooikrans glow reddish, and here anglers congregate above the sea to drop their lines almost vertically into deep water. Tunny (tuna) are usually taken from boats, but here they are hauled directly ashore, along with other catches. Another ledge, much lower down, is situated near Buffels Bay, where there are pools for swimming, and attractive picnic sites between thickets of milkwood. At another bathing place called Venus Pool there is an ancient lime kiln, situated in a remote setting, and much more so in the less settled days, when men collected shells and burnt them for the lime they used as a mortar and whitewash. Today, only a lazy, lacy spray drifts over the scene of their labours, making tiny rainbows in the sunlight.

Right: *Aerial view of Cape Point* (JM)

The Point

Tradition says that Cape Point is the meeting place of the warm Moçambique Current from the east, with the chilly Benguela Current that sweeps up from the far south. Scientists, however, say no, the real meeting place of the waters is much further to the east, in the vicinity of Cape Agulhas. Despite science, it is obvious to anyone who ventures into the water that the sea in False Bay is noticeably warmer than on the Atlantic or western side of the peninsula. And mists, a common phenomenon when warm and cold currents meet, are a frequent feature of Cape Point.

It was a mist that caused the loss of the fine Portuguese liner *Lusitania* in 1911. The low clouds hid the beam of the Cape Point lighthouse, and the *Lusitania* crashed bows-on into Bellows Rock and, by great good fortune, did not immediately slide off and sink. When she disappeared beneath the sea a few days later, everybody on board had been taken off, and the fate of the 'old' Cape Point lighthouse was sealed. It had been suggested 40 years earlier that the light be situated lower down, but it took this catastrophe to prompt the authorities into action. The base of this old lighthouse makes a good viewing platform, from where the sights include the 'new' lighthouse of 1914 – very much lower down.

Not even a lighthouse could have helped the ship, *Flying Dutchman*, that struggled against contrary winds to round the Cape, in about the year 1680. Cursing, her Captain called on Satan's aid, and swore he would round the Cape if it took him until Doomsday. And this, it is said, was the divine judgement that was passed on him, and that is why people still sometimes report seeing a battered old sailing ship struggling against the wind, only to disappear to the sound of maniacal laughter if she is hailed.

Right: *Cape Point lighthouse* (WK)

Cape Point
FAUNA

The name of Buffels Bay strongly suggests that buffalo once roamed the area that is now the Cape of Good Hope Nature Reserve. A visitor to this southern tip of the peninsula wrote, in 1829, that there were also 'porcupines, tigers, jackals and baboons'. The buffalo have gone, and so have the 'tigers' which, in reality, were not tigers at all, but probably leopards.

Now the stately, gentle eland walks the plains in peace, along with the rare bontebok, and the smaller springbok, grey rhebok and grysbok. The bontebok, with the bluebuck, used to roam the coastal plains of the Cape but, by 1800, the last bluebuck had been shot, and all that remains of it are travellers' descriptions and a pair of horns in the South African Museum in Cape Town. The same path to extinction lay ahead for the bontebok, until a few far-sighted farmers created a private reserve for this attractive, glossy-coated antelope. Even so, numbers were down to just 17 animals in the whole of South Africa – and therefore in the entire world – at one time. Now, though, their future seems assured.

Most visible of the animals of Cape Point are the baboons, of which there are five resident troops. Cut off by urban development from the rest of Africa, they have developed a lifestyle that probably makes them unique among the baboons of the world. Apart from the standard diet of roots, eggs, small reptiles and fruits, these baboons derive much of their food from the sea, gathering shellfish and whatever else they can find. Some have even been reported to have learned to scoop small fish out of rock pools. Despite warning signs, visitors feed the baboons, causing them to expect hand-outs from all humans. When their expectations are not met, they can become vicious and very destructive and, all because of misplaced kindness on the part of a thoughtless visitor, may have to be destroyed. It is advisable to keep a safe distance from baboons, especially when young animals are to be seen.

Legends of the baboons of Cape Point include the tale that when one has transgressed the law of the troop, it is tried before a court of its peers, assembled on the beach. It is said that they have been seen, in a noisy circle, barking and demonstrating around a solitary animal cringing in the centre. And the end of it all, attested to by more than one baboon, is that a verdict of guilty means that the doomed animal must plunge into the cold South Atlantic, there to perish in the breakers or in the jaws of sharks.

Much of the reserve used to be farmland, and when ostrich feathers became a popular and expensive fashion accessory about the middle of the 19th century, one of the local farmers, John McKellar, bought a breeding pair. Their descendants stalk the place to this day, and are often to be seen roaming Maclear Beach, a curious sight for any seaside. Other birds likely to be seen include the wheeling, majestic fish eagle and many other land species. Seabirds are abundant, and there are cormorants, black oystercatchers, gulls and gannet, plovers and sand-pipers.

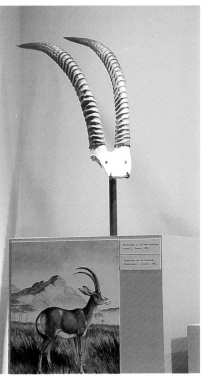

Left: *Bontebok* (JM)
Top right: *Black oystercatchers* (JH)
Top left: *Ostriches* (RJ)
Above: *Bluebuck horns at the South African Museum* (JH)

Cape Point
FLORA

One of the earliest descriptions of the area that is now the Cape of Good Hope Nature Reserve was left by a man who never saw it. Discharged from the British Royal Navy after being blinded in action, Lieutenant Holman nevertheless became a world traveller and, by the shrewd questions put to his various guides, became an accurate 'observer' through their eyes.

'Between the mountain ridge ... and Cape Point the plain is covered by an incredible number of ant hills, and mole hills, and there are a great variety of the proteas, mimosa, bulbs and beautiful heaths...' This is primarily *fynbos* country, where woody, evergreen shrubs predominate although, at just one point on the east coast near the peninsula's tip, there is a small stand of indigenous forest. It seems doubtful though, that the flora of the area, as a whole, ever looked much different to its appearance today.

Of the many floral species, some 13 grow only here, and nowhere else in the world, and are among the 30 species in the reserve that are endangered or considered rare. Here and there, exotic vegetation, mainly Australian in origin, has invaded this sanctuary, and efforts are maintained to root it out.

Among the few true tree species indigenous in the area is the white milkwood, *Sideroxylon inerme,* which characteristically grows close to the sea. It is a dense, leafy tree, sometimes assuming no more than shrub-like proportions because, here at the Cape of Storms, violent winds may twist it into fantastic shapes. The white milkwood, in any case, rarely does grow very straight, but it does grow very old. If you should visit Mossel Bay on the Garden Route you will see the Post Office Tree, a gnarled white milkwood that is at least 600 years old. None in the reserve is thought to be as old as this, but they have been sheltering their colonies of birds for many years.

The Cape of Good Hope Nature Reserve has been described, and correctly, as 'Cape Town's biggest natural wild-flower garden', and it offers its flowers in varieties, from winter fields bright with red-hot poker *(Kniphofia* species) to little rocky outcrops where red crassula cling in the crevices.

Above and below: *Cape of Good Hope Nature Reserve* (ER)

Although spring is the peak of the flowering season, the blooms of autumn are still plentiful and rewarding. There are the nerines that, through the accident of shipwreck (see p69) have become known to the world as Guernsey lilies, and white Harveya or inkblom. White Harveya is really a very pale pink, and it is called inkblom because, when the petals are crushed or bruised, they look as though they have been stained with ink. The blue disa, related to the red disa of Table Mountain, is an autumn-flowering orchid of Cape Point, where the giant proteas also flourish.

In only one small, hilly part of the reserve will you find Dod's Staavia (*Staavia dodii*), a dense little shrub that, in winter and early spring, is covered with little bright white flowers with a dark purple centre. It is appropriate that in this treasure-house of plants, the local people call it simply 'Diamond Eyes'.

Below: *Diosanthemum speciosum* (KP)

Simon's Town

To generations of Royal Navy men Simon's Town was known as Snoekie, and this was the base of the South Atlantic squadron from 1814, until the naval facilities were transferred to the South African Navy in 1957. There are several lovely beaches south of Simon's Town, the closest of which is adjacent to the town, at Boulders, where great mounds of granite provide shelter on windy days. With bathing done, there is much to see in the town.

An old parsonage, in which the music was composed for the South African national anthem, serves as the Museum for National Symbols, which comprises an extensive collection of flags and other examples of heraldry. In the squat and stone-built Martello Tower is a collection of naval relics, especially those that tell the story of the growth of the South African Navy. Jubilee Square has its anchors and cannons as befitting a naval town, and a fine statue of Able Seaman Just Nuisance, the legendary dog that adopted – and officially joined – the Royal Navy during World War II. Even the old historic cemetery gives a graphic idea of the lives and times of ships and men long gone, recording deaths of a warship and her crew.

The Old Residency of 1772, now houses the Simon's Town Museum and is a fascinating place in which to while away the hours. There's more here on sea-dog Just Nuisance, there are guns and swords and all manner of memorabilia, including the reconstructed 'Africa Station Club' with its cosy bar and allegedly ghostly picture. Nearby St Francis church has had strong associations with the Royal Navy since its consecration in 1837. Many West African 'kroo-men' served with the navy and have their monuments here, alongside those commemorating more exalted ranks. The 'kroo-men', though, are remembered by the names that the navy gave them, presumably being unable to pronounce their real names. So here you see memorials to Tom Cockroach, Bottle of Beer, Jack Ropeyarn and others.

Top: *Statue of Just Nuisance, Jubilee Square* (ER)
Right: *Simon's Town harbour* (GC)

Simon's Town, named for 17th century Governor van der Stel, is the terminus of the railway from Cape Town. A trip along the stretch of rail from Simon's Town to Muizenberg, running so close to the sea that spray is sometimes blown over the coaches, is well worth the cost of the ticket. Lying forlornly off Long Beach, and a useful resting place for gulls and cormorants, is the steam engine of the *Clan Stuart*, which dragged its anchors and went aground in 1914.

Right: *Inside the Simon's Town Museum* (GC)
Far right: *Boulder's beach* (ER)

Fish Hoek

There was a distant time, scientists say, when the sea flowed across the Cape Flats, and the Cape Peninsula was not just one island, but two. The sea also cut across the peninsula, from Fish Hoek on the west side, over the flat, sandy plain of Fish Hoek Valley, to the wide Noordhoek beaches. If the sea level were to rise by just 30 metres, it would all happen again.

Fish Hoek, oddly enough, is famous for being a 'dry' town, although it is orientated around the sea. When Governor Lord Charles Somerset proclaimed the area a fishery in 1818, he made it a condition that no 'public winehouse' should be kept here, and that the right to fish should be free. Despite sporadic grumblings, the conditions are still in force in the Municipality of Fish Hoek to this day.

The mountains above Fish Hoek and Kalk Bay are riddled with caves that the adventurous delight in exploring. These are not for the claustrophobic though, as some are extremely narrow, with ceilings of rock so low that you need to wriggle to get by. Boomslang Cave which, apart from being a tight squeeze in places, also has a stretch of very chilly water to be waded through, has one opening on the northerly slopes and another on the south. Harry's Hollow, Squeezer's Cave and Dread Halls are some of the others.

It is from a cave on a ridge a short way inland from Fish Hoek, that we know, that primitive man ventured out to hunt the game that must have been plentiful here some 10 000 years ago. Perhaps the sea even at that time lapped close to his ever-open hearth. A local man and his son excavated the cave in the 1920s, moving and removing tons of earth and fallen rock, and found a number of fossilized skeletons that have been classed as ancestral to the Khoisan or Bushman people. The cave is called Skildersgat, because there used to be rock paintings to be seen there, or Peers Cave, after its excavators, and is open to the public.

Top: *Aerial view of Fish Hoek* (JH)
Right: *Fish Hoek from Silvermine Nature Reserve* (GC)

Also up on the plateau, from where there are beautiful views over False Bay, is the Silvermine Nature Reserve. Picnic sites are dotted about under shady pines, and many bird species are attracted to the nectar of a wide variety of indigenous flowers that include protea, leucadendron and erica. Why 'silvermine'? If you know where to look along the road called Ou Kaapse Weg, you'll find just that, a silver mine. Actually, there are three workings in all, dating from the 1680s, but it is doubtful if any silver was ever found here or at a few other places that were being worked on the peninsula at that time. It all seems to have been a swindle on the part of the Dutch East India Company's resident miner who, in the end, was 'arrested and locked in the Castle' before being shipped off to Sumatra in the East Indies.

Below: *Fish Hoek from the beach* (JM)

False Bay

Mariners sailing home to Europe from the East not infrequently mistook the eastern bulk of Cape Hangklip for the Cape of Good Hope itself, at the western side of the bay. This was especially so in poor visibility, leading the navigator to give the order to change to a northerly course which, within a few hours, brought his ship perilously close to the beach at Muizenberg. So far as is known, no ship was actually wrecked because of this wrong manoeuvre, but it happened so often that the name of False Cape was given to Hangklip, and was also applied to the great inlet as False Bay.

The bay is well protected from the north-west winds that did so much damage to shipping in Table Bay before an adequate breakwater was built, and it was recommended in the 17th century as a safe winter anchorage. A mixed running and sailing battle was fought from Simon's Town to Muizenberg in 1795 between ships of the Royal Navy and Dutch and local soldiers. Ships of the line, including *Stately*, *American* and *Rattlesnake*, cruised majestically parallel to the shore, cannonading the defenders. From a battery at Muizenberg the Dutch were able to score a few hits, and old cannons at the bowling club there are thought to have been used in the battle. In the end, the British duly occupied the Cape settlement.

A good view of the places where the action occurred is to be had from the high-level road, Boyes Drive, between Lakeside and Kalk Bay. The view is panoramic, and takes in the entire sweep of the bay and the distant Hottentots Holland Mountains on the eastern shore. Below, too, is the busy fishing harbour of Kalk Bay, where an especially attractive, thatch-roofed church offers cool sanctuary from worldly bustle.

Previous page: *Cape Town in the early evening from Signal Hill* (MvA)

Top: *The beach and bathing boxes at St James* (MvA)
Middle: *The pathway from St James to Muizenberg* (ER)
Right: *St James* (ER)

The False Bay coast was once a popular place for the mining magnates of the Transvaal to build their seaside homes, and an interesting contrast is to be seen in Muizenberg. There's the little thatched cottage in which Cecil John Rhodes died in 1902. Immediately south of it is a huge, double-storeyed home in the style known as Cape Dutch Revival, called Rust en Vrede, built a few years later as the home of Rhodes' friend, Sir Abe Bailey. Bailey also had his cottage, just across the railway line, and Bailey's Cottage is a well-known fishing spot along this coastline.

Another elegant home is The Fort, now an exhibition venue of the South African National Gallery, and there are other old and interesting houses along the seafront. Many of these can be seen from a paved pathway, wedged between railway line and sea, which provides a delightful walk between St James and Muizenberg beach. Muizenberg Pavilion, on the other hand, is designed for the '90s. It is a focus for restaurants, playing parks, water sports and exhibitions. The popular resort of St James has changed little in the past half-century. The small, sandy bay is still lined with brightly painted, wooden changing cubicles, locally called bathing boxes. The safe tidal pool of St James is an added attraction along this coastline.

Tokai

Deep within sighing pine plantations is one of the more unusual jewels of Cape-Dutch architecture, the splendidly sited homestead of Tokai, now the residence of the warden of a nearby boys' reformatory. The house was built in the 1790s, but its owner lavished so much money on its construction that he enjoyed living in it for only a very short time before being declared insolvent. At around New Year, and only at midnight, a headless man is said to ride a horse across the lawn and up one of the curving flights of steps to the high stoep.

An arboretum next to the old house features numerous indigenous and exotic trees, and a helpful botanical information centre. On the slopes of Constantiaberg, behind the house, is a cave known as Elephant's Eye because of its position on an outline that looks roughly like the back and head of an elephant. It is also known as Prinseskasteel, because of a legend that it was once the home of a Khoikhoi princess.

Wynberg

Wynberg, where the Dutch founder of the settlement, Jan van Riebeeck, successfully grew wine grapes, was later the home of a large transient population known to the locals as 'Indians'. These were British military personnel and civil servants from the vast establishment in India, and they came to the Cape to recuperate from illness or for relief from the glaring Indian summers. After the opening of the Suez Canal in 1869, and the consequently much shorter passage home to England, the numbers dropped somewhat, but the old part of Wynberg, sometimes known as Little Chelsea, still has many picturesque residences that were temporary homes for generations of empire-builders.

One of Wynberg's open spaces is Maynardville, where an annual Community Carnival is held to raise funds for charity. Maynardville also sees, in summer, a season of Shakespeare, with plays performed in an enchanting outdoor theatre, where 'players glide into our consciousness from night's velvety blackness, and transport the audience into a world of sheer magic'. Equally far in spirit from the bustle of city life are the lawns and shady, bird-haunted trees of Wynberg Park.

Above: *Restored house in 'Little Chelsea', Wynberg* (GC)
Top: *Tokai Manor House* (JS)

Constantia

The farm Groot Constantia was created by Governor Simon van der Stel in the late 17th century, and it is believed that he loved it so much that he has never left it. The walks and halls are said to be haunted by a most amiable ghost, and even today there is certainly an air of serenity and constancy, in and around this most classic of Cape-Dutch estates. The wine cellar behind the house features an intricately carved and entertaining pediment, depicting the legend of Ganymede, most beautiful of mortals who was carried off by the gods to serve as their wine-bearer.

Wines of Constantia were famous centuries ago, and are said to have consoled the Emperor Napoleon in his lonely exile on the island of St. Helena. Excellent wines are still made here, and are available on the estate, where there are also restaurants and a wine museum in the old cellar. Note the layout of the major buildings, with the cellar behind the homestead instead of being placed symmetrically opposite the jonkershuis, as at Boschendal and Lanzerac (see p74). The only explanation for this deviation from the standard arrangement must be that it preserved the magnificent view over green vines to the distant curve of False Bay.

Top: *Stone church, Tokai* (JH)
Right: *Tokai forest* (JMc)

Groote Schuur

At the grave of Cecil John Rhodes in the Matopo Hills of Zimbabwe there is only a bronze plaque to mark the spot. But here on his former Groote Schuur estate his friend and architect, Herbert Baker, raised to his memory a miniature Grecian temple in one of the most impressive settings to be found anywhere in the world. The four pairs of bronze lions were sculpted by G F Watts, who also created the main group, 'Energy', in which the horseman has his face turned to the north, Rhodes' 'hinterland'. The hill on which the memorial stands was one of Rhodes' favourite spots, where he used to sit and admire the view as he dreamed his dreams of empire.

The main campus of the University of Cape Town – which had its beginnings as the South African College in 1829 – is also situated on the Groote Schuur estate. The older buildings, of Table Mountain sandstone, were first occupied in 1928, but, since then, the university has expanded greatly, and many more, modern-idiom buildings have been added. In front of the campus, with its statue of Rhodes seated, and just across the De Waal Drive, is the 18th century summerhouse of Rustenburg, where the old Cape governors spent the hot months of summer away from the heat and bustle of the Castle.

Above Newlands, a little to the south of the university, forests of pine and eucalyptus shade the scant remains of a cottage called Paradise. Here, when their duties at the Castle permitted it, Lady Anne Barnard and her husband, the Colonial Secretary, also slipped the bonds of officialdom and escaped to a scene of tranquillity that was, around 1800, quite far out in the country. Now the forest plantations are the haunt of picnickers and joggers, and families out for a stroll in what is still a pretty spot if not quite paradise.

Rhodes's house, which he bequeathed as the home of prime ministers of a united South Africa – a reality that still lay in the future at the time of his death – was once just a storage barn: the 'groote schuur'. Its present appearance, though, dates from the turn of the century when, after a fire, it was rebuilt to the design of Herbert Baker in the Cape-Dutch Revival style.

Above: *Valkenberg* (JS)
Top: *Groote Schuur* (JS)

Above right: *University of Cape Town* (ER)
Right: *Early evening view from Rhodes' Memorial*
(MvA)

There was an 'onder schuur' too, and this 'lower barn' has also undergone a Cinderella-like transformation into a stately home, although perhaps with less pleasing effect than Groote Schuur. Now named Westbrooke, after a 19th century owner, it is another of the official State residences that cluster around Groote Schuur. Still on Rhodes' estate, but somewhat to the north, is Groote Schuur Hospital where, in 1967, world medical news was made with the first human heart transplant. The old hospital of 1938, with a façade that loyally depicts elements of Cape-Dutch, still perches on its windy hill. Below it, in uncompromisingly modern style, is the new hospital of the 1980s, sprawling box-like above an area where several generations of medical students have traditionally had their 'digs' in little terraced houses.

Mostert's Mill
and The Liesbeeck River

Early settler Cornelis Botmas obviously found contentment in this part of the world, and named his allotment Welgelegen – well situated. Here, in a much later year, about 1796, was built the windmill that still stands on Welgelegen, between the old threshing floor and the highway that was once Cecil Rhodes' private driveway from the city to his estate. Old Dirk van Reenen and Mostert the miller, who built the mill, would be surprised at the cars flashing by, but they would be pleased to note that their mill is still in perfect working order. Successive owners of Welgelegen rest in the little white-walled cemetery below the Rhodes Memorial.

There used to be many mills in the vicinity of old Cape Town, but few remain. On the Liesbeeck River in Newlands, just below Main Road, is Josephine Mill. The restored water-wheel again turns the millstones, so grinding flour for fascinated visitors, at the headquarters of the Cape Town Historical Society. There is another restored windmill near Durbanville, in the northern suburbs.

The Liesbeeck, having turned the wheel of the Josephine Mill, flows on down through the suburb of Observatory, where there is another rare survivor – a farmhouse in the city. This is Valkenburg, which stood empty and decayed almost to ruination before it was restored to unexpected glory in the 1980s. Now a restaurant, this was one of the farms allotted to the first Free Burghers, in 1661, and the homestead in its present form probably dates from the late 18th century, with a rare curvilinear parapet on the north wing. Nearby is Valkenburg mill, sadly dilapidated and barely recognizable.

Another fascinating place along the Liesbeeck River, that can be visited by appointment, is the South African Astronomical Observatory, where buildings and records date back for over 150 years. The observatory gave its name to the suburb and, because of close historic associations, the Union Jack of Great Britain flies here alongside the flag of South Africa.

Right: *Mostert's Mill* (ER)

Below: *Valkenburg* (JH)
Above: *Josephine Mill* (ER)

Markets and Festivals

Lawrence Green, an author who loved this city, once wrote that 'it seems that the soul of Cape Town moves with the troubadours and their music'. (*see* picture p59) The Coon Carnival is perhaps the oldest expression of street music, of spontaneous song and dance and high spirits, still to be seen in Cape Town. Some say it has its origins far back with the end of slavery in the 1830s, others that it dates only from the visit of an American minstrel troupe in 1887. Certainly, the first organized carnival was held in 1906, and it has been an annual tradition ever since, vibrant with colour and, indeed, a part of 'the soul of Cape Town'.

The site of the original fort, now the Grand Parade, holds another tradition; here a diversity of market stalls are set up bi-weekly. There are permanent kiosks, too, where you may buy fruit and vegetables, or quench your thirst, but this was a parade ground as long ago as 1697. The men of Dutch, French, British and South African regiments have 'fallen in' here, with colours flying, drums beating and the flash of sunlight bright on the barrage of bayonets. This, too, is Cape Town's traditional open-air venue for political gatherings, from a demonstration in 1849 to protest against the establishment of a convict settlement, to the vast gathering in 1990 to hear Nelson Mandela make his first public speech on his release after 27 years of imprisonment.

A guide book of 1858, says that the Grand Parade 'is to the Cape folk what market days are in England' and goes on to list some of the goods to be found for sale there – 'clearings-out of warehouses, sea captains' adventures, damaged cargoes, furniture, china, plate, crockery, hardware, paintings and engravings, eatables, perfumery, clothes, tools, seeds, trees, horses and carts, carriages and harness...' Not all these goods are common on today's market, but clothes, haberdashery, hardware and flowers are just some of the merchandise still to be found here.

Top: *Festival lights in Adderley Street* (ER)
Middle: *Dutch dancing at the Cape Festival* (JH)
Right: *Old Town House, Greenmarket Square* (JM)
Far right: *Greenmarket Square* (JM)

It is not just the Grand Parade that is a market-place. In high summer, and during the Cape Festival and on Saturdays throughout the year, traders spread their wares in many places. Outside the railway station is a favourite pitch, but perhaps the most picturesque is the market that hums and buzzes on Greenmarket Square. The façade of the Old Town House (which houses a fine collection of old Dutch Masters) looks down on a sea of canopies and stalls spread like a maze and threaded with knots and lines of people come to buy or, most of them, just to see what is on offer.

The Cape Town Festival encourages exploration of the city and peninsula, of the museums and galleries, and invites participation in the goings-on to be found almost anywhere. Cape Town exists because of the sea, and the tendency is to try to get Capetonians and their visitors back to their historic roots. For this reason, the old dockland of the Victoria and Albert basins has more than ever to offer at this time.

Above: *Coon Carnival* (ER)
Right: *The station market* (JM)
Below: *Street market in Claremont* (GC)

Cape Town
Entertainment & Culture

Our early Dutch colonists considered many light entertainments frivolous, so it is not surprising that the colony's first theatre was opened only in 1802 – under the Cape's temporary period of British administration. It served as a theatre for more than 30 years before public opinion closed it down, to re-open as a church. And St Steven's Church, formerly the African Theatre, still stands on Riebeeck Square. Public opinion has undergone some enlightenment since those times, and entertainment, whether frivolous or otherwise, abounds in the city.

There's a different character to each of the major play-houses, in their distinctive settings. There's the Nico Malan Theatre and Opera House, home of the Cape Performing Arts Board, set amid lawns on the wide – and sometimes windy – Foreshore. From soloists to full-scale grand opera or ballet, here are venues to accommodate all forms of the performing arts. Squirreled oaks surround the functional lines of the Baxter Theatre in Rondebosch, while at the Theatre on the Bay in Camps Bay you can while away the interval by sipping drinks on the roof and hearing the soft soughing of the sea.

The Little Theatre on the Orange Street campus of the University of Cape Town is also a venue for varied productions and, scattered about the peninsula, you'll find other theatres or halls that are used by amateur groups of surprising competence. And Maynardville (*see* p52), of course, is that most special setting for Shakespeare in summer, and for a annual charity festival, where if you're lucky you may be able to see a performance of the mystic Khalifa, with incense and thudding drums a brooding background to the icy flash of sword and skewer.

Top: *Baxter Theatre, Rondebosch* (JM)
Right: *Art in St George's Mall* (JH)

Right: *Theatre on the Bay, Camps Bay* (JM)

Cape Town has its music too, from the itinerant street-corner flautist or penny-whistle exponent to the formality of the Cape Town Symphony Orchestra, which has been maintained as a civic amenity since 1914. Many and famous have been its guest conductors down the years since then. There are small concerts too, at times, held amid the classic elegance of some old building that has held music for centuries. The Old Town House on Greenmarket Square, where hangs the Michaelis Collection of Dutch old masters, is one such musical venue.

Art galleries abound, sometimes in combination with antique dealerships, and exhibitions are frequent. Apart from the very comprehensive collections in the South African National Gallery in the Company's Gardens, there are galleries throughout the city, but especially along narrow Church Street where, on occasion, stall-holders add to the scene with their assorted wares of yesteryear.

Museums too, bring yesteryear to life, and those that display include the South African Cultural History Museum in Adderley Street, at the foot of Government Avenue. This rather grand old building was developed from the old Company's slave lodge, and served as the meeting place for the first colonial governments before housing their Supreme Court. Now its cool interior, seemingly far removed from the bustle outside its substantial walls, displays the gracious artefacts of the country's past. Related museums are Koopmans De Wet House in Strand Street, a perfectly preserved town residence of the late 18th century, Bertram House at the top (south) end of Government Avenue, which a wealthy English colonist built and furnished so as to create the illusion that he was still in England. In Wale Street, where it enters Bo-Kaap, is the Bo-Kaap Museum housed in a delightful dwelling with a scrolled front parapet undoubtedly built by one of the inimitable Malay craftsmen whose old home is faithfully re-created inside. A maritime museum is being developed in the harbour area to display the rich sea-going heritage of the city. In the harbour old ships are afloat – the boom defence vessel SAS *Somerset* and the old steam tug, *Alwyn Vincent,* are moored alongside one another. Off Portswood Road, nearby, narrow Fort Wynyard Road leads to the Fort Wynyard Museum of coastal and anti-aircraft artillery. This 19th century fort was manned during the Second World War as one of the important Table Bay defences.

1. *South African National Gallery* (JH)
2. *South African Natural History Museum* (JH)
3. *Koopmans de Wet House, Strand Street* (JH)
4. *Inside the Bo-Kaap Museum, Wale Street* (JH)
5. *Bertram House, Government Avenue* (JH)

Restaurants

Dining is one of the chief delights of Cape Town, greatly influenced by the national tastes and delicate touches brought by a population that has its roots over more than half the world. And with the bounteous seas at its doorstep, the Tavern of the Seas, as old Cape Town was known, is famous for its seafood dishes. The places where you can sample Cape cooking are many, and many are justly renowned, from the formal starch and candlelight of a famous hotel to the alfresco spread of a country manor. To some places you may go as much for the music as the food, according to whether you prefer jazz or baroque, and the dainties appropriate to each. There are international dishes aplenty, but take time to sample also bredie and blatjang, sambal and smoorvis. These are just a few of the dishes of the Cape, and you may not find them anywhere else in the world.

World of Birds

Great walk-through cages of concentrated colour and birdsong await you at Hout Bay's World of Birds wildlife sanctuary. So vast are the cages that there is no impression whatever of the birds being enclosed, and they seem to be in their wild and natural state. Now accustomed to humans at close range, many are remarkably tame, and will pose happily for close-up photographs.

In his standard work, *Birds of South Africa*, Austin Roberts rightly describes the sight of a Knysna lourie in flight as 'almost a tourist attraction'; it is indeed a rare privilege. The wonderful spread of red as it opens its wings can readily be seen at the World of Birds.

In all, there are close to 4 000 birds of more than 300 species, of both indigenous and exotic specimens. This sanctuary was established in the 1970s, and the proprietor receives birds in a great variety of ways, be it from a neighbourhood child with an injured pigeon, or an airborne consignment of flamingo chicks abandoned by their parents when the rains failed in faraway Namibia.

1

2

3

4

5

1. *Chestnut mandible* (HvJ)
2. *Snowy owl* (HvJ)
3. *White-faced whistling duck* (HvJ)
4. *Inside one of the enclosures* (JH)
5. *Giant eagle owl* (HvJ)
6. *Gymnogene* (HvJ)
7. *Knysna loerie* (JH)
8. *Sacred ibis* (HvJ)
9. *Lilac-breasted roller* (HvJ)
10. *Blue and gold macaw* (JH)
11. *Blue crane* (HvJ)
12. *Little egret* (HvJ)
13. *Lady Amherst pheasant* (HvJ)
(Identified by Mr Cloete from The World of Birds)

As far as possible, natural environments have been faithfully created for the different types of birds, so that they go about the business of living their daily lives unafraid. A number of species that find shelter at World of Birds are on the endangered list, and include jackass penguin, Cape vulture, brown-headed parrot and white pelican.

There are creatures other than birds, too, like the little, friendly monkeys, dozy and round-eyed bushbabies, mongooses, dassies and tortoises. A visit is more than interesting for adults, and more than exciting for children.

Kirstenbosch

At Kirstenbosch there are flowers to greet the visitor at any season of the year, from the daisies, mesembryanthemums and annuals in spring, to the proteas and ericas that show their stately blooms in winter. Kirstenbosch covers an area of more than 500 hectares, of which little more than ten per cent is cultivated, the remainder being a natural flora reserve.

A history of planting here goes back more than 300 years, to 1660, when Commander Jan van Riebeeck planted a hedge of indigenous wild almond *(Brabejum stellatifolium)* to mark the limits of his settlement. Some of his trees may still be seen, a number of them within the boundary of Kirstenbosch itself. Unfortunately, the settlers also cut down a great number of trees, for repairs to ships and for building. Late in the 19th century, much of the mountain slope between Rondebosch and Constantia Nek was purchased by Cecil John Rhodes from the farmer and former soldier, Johann Kirsten. Rhodes intended to create a public parkland with this area, but after his death, in 1902, the land passed to government ownership, in trust for the people of South Africa.

The National Botanic Gardens of South Africa were created by an Act of Parliament in 1913, to study, cultivate and preserve the plants of this country. Kirstenbosch was the first of these gardens, and more have been established in the other provinces, each specializing in the local flora. At Kirstenbosch, for instance, are to be found some 2 000 of the 20 000 plant species indigenous to South Africa. Almost half of the Cape Peninsula's flora species grow here, readily accessible to all who love their varied and fragile beauty.

Apart from the routes that lead to the high-lying parts of Kirstenbosch, all paths are smoothly surfaced, and each radiates to a special section where related plant groups are

Above: *Kirstenbosch* (ER)

Middle left: *Mesembryanthemums* (ER)
Middle right: *Mesembryanthemums* (ER)
Right: *Sugar bird on Leucospermum* (ER)

Right: *The pond at Kirstenbosch* (ER)
Middle left: *Protea aristata* (ER)
Middle right: *The Braille Garden* (ER)

cultivated together, and include the Cycad Amphitheatre, Protea Garden and bright-covered Pelargonium Koppie. A Fragrance Garden of indigenous aromatic plants, and a Braille Trail are specially designed for the blind or poorly sighted, and have labels in braille as well as in extra-large type. The Silver Tree Stroll and Weaver Bird Walk lead along level paths suitable for wheelchairs and prams.

An important part of the work of the gardens is done indoors, in the Compton Herbarium, where scientific procedures include the classification and analysis of South African flora, of which the herbarium possesses more than 250 000 specimens. This total is second only to that in the National Herbarium in Pretoria, and includes specimens collected as long ago as 1825. Sad to relate, a number of species represented in these collections have become extinct. The herbarium is open on weekdays and may be visited by appointment only.

An information office at the entrance is open every day, and a selection of plants and seeds may be bought. Kirstenbosch is the headquarters of the Botanical Society of South Africa, which maintains an office and bookshop. At the restaurant, refreshments may be taken indoors or, on idyllic summer days, in the shade of the oaks. This is a favourite spot for Sunday breakfasts and birthday celebrations.

Lower middle left: *Strelitzia* (ER)
Lower middle right: *Protea caffra* (ER)
Right: *Spring colours in Kirstenbosch* (ER)

Almost all visitors to Kirstenbosch are fascinated by the cycads. After all, there is something extraordinary about plants that have been in existence for almost 300 million years. The fossil record shows that cycads, virtually unchanged from those that grow today, flourished when dinosaurs were the dominant life form on earth. There are three families of cycads, with *Encephalartos* being the commonest in South Africa, where there are about 25 species. It is also called the 'breadfruit tree', because the pith from the stems yields a nutritious starch that can be ground to form flour. The seed cones may weigh as much as 30 kilograms or more, and many of the seeds themselves are poisonous. The fleshy, outer layer of many species is edible and tasty, but the kernel may be poisonous, and cycad seeds are known to have caused the death of cattle that grazed them. Although the cycads have survived for so long, they are, in fact, slowly becoming extinct, and there were very many more different varieties in the days of the dinosaurs. The Cycad Amphitheatre was established by the first director of Kirstenbosch, Professor H W Pearson, who collected several hundred specimens, most of them from the eastern Cape Province. He wrote of them in his report for 1915, that 'This collection is one of which any of the great botanic gardens of the world might well be proud'. All species of cycads are protected in South Africa and Zimbabwe.

Many Cape flowers belong to the daisy family, or Compositae. The name 'daisy' comes from Old English, and means 'day's eye', from the flower's resemblance to a radiant sunburst of colour. The Namaqualand daisy that, with a host of other flowers, transforms the dry veld in springtime, is *Arctotis fastuosa*, but the best known daisy of the Cape is the white raindaisy, *Dimorphotheca pluvialis*. It is a Cape Town tradition that, in years when the slopes of Signal Hill are covered by a dense, snow-like carpet of rain-daisies in late winter, that an excellent flower season will follow. These are among the many daisy species that greet the spring with shining, colourful flowers at Kirstenbosch.

Many members of the large family of mesembryanthems are to be seen here. Their name means 'noon flower', because they open fully when the sun is at its height. Visitors from the south of England will recognize many mesems as flowers that grow wild in Devon and Cornwall, where they have been grown for about two hundred years. In Portugal and as far

Above left: *Leucospermum vestitum* (ER)
Above right: *Blushing bride* (ER)
Below left: *Erica nana* (ER)
Below right: *Haemanthus coccineus* (ER)
Bottom: *Encephalartos* (ER)

away as Australia and California, countries where the mesem has become naturalized, local people refer to them as Hottentot figs, and they are generally known in South Africa as 'vygies'. To the folk of Cornwall, they are known as 'Sally my handsome', while on the Scilly Isles they have been called 'mesmerisms'. They belong to the genus *Carpobrotus*, succulents that seem to thrive in almost any soil, asking only for a shower or two between autumn and spring. Very closely related is the Bokbaaivygie (*Dorotheanthus*), originally found growing in poor seasand just above the tide line on the western Cape coast.

It may seem surprising to find the Guernsey lily (*Nerine sarniensis*) flourishing in a garden that is supposed to be devoted to indigenous South African plants, but the mountains of the south-western Cape Province are, in fact, its natural home. The case of mistaken identity arose because in 1659, a Dutch ship on its way home to Holland from Japan, after calling at the Cape, was wrecked on one of the Channel Islands. Boxes of Cape bulbs washed ashore on the island of Guernsey, took root and, in due course, produced their delicate, scarlet flowers. Eventually, enterprising islanders exported them to florists all over Europe, and the bulbs were thought to be natives of Japan, where the wrecked ship had come from. (Another case of mistaken botanical identity through shipwreck concerns the Scarborough lily, which is really a native of the southern Cape, *Cyrtanthus purpureus* or, as it is more commonly known here, the George lily).

A measure of the reputation of Kirstenbosch, not just in South Africa, but in the world, was revealed in the 1970s, when it was proposed to build an elevated, six-lane freeway across the entrance to the gardens. Letters of protest poured in, from people in all occupations, as well as botanists. In his eloquent protest, Professor Richard A Howard of Harvard University's Arnold Arboretum wrote: 'Kirstenbosch is the distinguished creation of a dedicated people, and from it has come a body of knowledge, published contributions and shared beauty that ranks Kirstenbosch at the very top of the world's botanic gardens.'

Above: *Euphorbia cooperi* (ER)
Below left: *Leucadendron* (ER)
Below right: *Protea cynaroides* (ER)

The Winelands

Constantia

When Governor Simon van der Stel ran the estate, given to him by the Dutch East India Company, it was called Constantia. After his death in 1712, it was divided into three parts, known as Groot Constantia, Klein Constantia and Bergvliet. The present name of this Klein Constantia is Hoop-op-Constantia, not to be confused with the later Klein Constantia, of about 1790.

The oak-shaded hills and valleys of Constantia are the real cradle of the South African wine industry. The first wine, it is true, was produced from grapes grown on nearby Wynberg Hill, but it is not recorded as being of particularly good quality. Wine continued to be made and, when opinion as to quality was recorded, it was generally unfavourable. Then came Commander Simon van der Stel, he who loved oak trees and, at heart, was probably more a farmer than an administrator. And at what is now Groot Constantia he set out to establish a model farm, with the emphasis on the production of high-quality wines from model vineyards.

His was not the only estate to produce wine in this serene place of grapes and gables. Buitenverwachting with its high stoep and impressive façade, dates from 1796. Vegetables were grown here until recently but, since the mid-1980s, the fine wines of Buitenverwachting have again been available. Stately Alphen also produced wines on its estate before land vanished under urban encroachment, and there are other estates and homesteads, each with its own story of time and constancy.

Top: *Groot Constantia* (JH)
Right: *The pool at Groot Constantia* (ER)
Far right: *The new cellar, Groot Constantia* (JM)

Above: *Constantia vines* (JH)
Right: *Barrel-making at Groot Constantia* (ER)
Below: *Klein Constantia winery* (ER)

Stellenbosch

It was in 1679, that Commander Simon van der Stel, newly appointed to govern the Cape settlement, visited the fertile valley of the Eerste River and decided to establish here a new agricultural settlement. The names of the earliest farms of the new district included Ida's Valley, Coetzenburg, Koelenhof, Kromme Rivier, Rustenburg, Jonkershoek and Spier. Some produce wine to this day, and all were in existence by the time the town itself was founded in 1685.

The old Commander named the place after himself. Formerly it had been De Wilde Bosch – 'the wild forest' – now it became Van der Stels-bosch, or Stellenbosch. One can forgive him his little vanity, because it was always his intention to combine settlement and nature as harmoniously as possible and, even today, the town retains its old air of rural elegance in the heart of its winelands. After Cape Town, it is the oldest town in South Africa and, after Constantia, the oldest wine-producing district.

While worthy traditions are respected and retained, there is much progress, too, in the use of increasingly sophisticated equipment. Machines may be used for harvesting and gently crushing the grapes, and computers for monitoring the age-old process of fermentation. For the most part, though, picking the grapes is done by hand, in the cool hours just before and after sunrise. Stainless steel is indeed used in some wineries but, unlike wood, it is merely a container and has no life or nuance that it can impart to the wine.

The Stellenbosch countryside is not entirely given over to the vine, and roadside farm stalls offer a surprising variety of fruits and preserves, juices and handicrafts. And the countryside in itself is an attraction, with curving gable and mellow thatch complementing the sterner line of mountain and the soft swell of hillsides.

Stellenbosch is where wines are born – in small cellars tended by just a few dedicated acolytes or – increasingly, in co-operatives or in even larger combines where the wine-maker has become scientist, without losing his intimate and personal association with his product. Oude Libertas is the headquarters of such a concern, Stellenbosch Farmers' Winery, which was started, curiously enough, by a Kentucky medical doctor who arrived in South

Above: *Oude Nektar* (ER)
Below left: *Vineyards of Stellenbosch* (ER)
Below right: *The tranquility of the Stellenbosch surrounds* (JM)
Bottom: *Van Ryn Brandy Cellar, Vlottenburg* (ER)

Africa by sea at the turn of the century, in charge of a batch of horses destined for the British Army.

The name Libertas goes back to when the land belonged to Adam Tas, the scurrilous diarist, who was thrown into the dungeons of the Castle (*see* p8) in 1706, for organizing a petition against the governor, who was none other than the son of Simon van der Stel. When Tas was released after more than a year, he returned to the farm and celebrated the occasion, it is said, by re-naming it Libertas – Tas is free. It makes a good story but, like so many others, is just not true. The farm was already named Libertas when he acquired it through marriage to the widow of its former owner, but the name, on his release, must have taken on a special significance.

Stellenbosch has retained some fine old traditions, along with the centuries-old oaks that line its streets of cool, white houses. The craft and traditions of the cooper seemed doomed to extinction in an age of plastics and aseptic stainless steel, but wine is a natural product that requires intimate contact with natural surroundings – such as the casks of imported French oak. And so the ancient trade was revived, and thrives again as, with simple, traditional tools, casks are made as they were made when Stellenbosch was very young.

Lanzerac was known as Schoongezicht when it was granted to Isaac Schrijver in 1692, when the town was only seven years old. Schrijver had been a sergeant of the marines, and had led pioneering expeditions to Namaqualand and the far Karoo before he retired to his Schoongezicht, or 'lovely view', in 1699. The present house, with its ornate, pilaster gables and cool floors of Batavian tiles, dates from about 1830. Lanzerac has been a hotel for some years, although a delightful rosé wine, in a dewdrop-shaped bottle, is still marketed under its name.

North-east of Stellenbosch, the Simonsberg rises to a height of 1 454 metres, jagged and massive. Somewhere on the slopes is a mine, relic of South Africas' first private mining venture where, in 1743, shafts were sunk in the belief that a valuable lode of silver was awaiting easy recovery. Silver-mining was a popular venture in early South African history, but never succeeded.

Over to the west is the lower outline of Papegaaisberg, the 'parrot mountain'. The name dates from the late 17th century, when the burghers of Stellenbosch held an annual fair, attended by their patron and governor, Simon van der Stel. Part of the day's fun included shooting at the wooden silhouette of a parrot, mounted so as to swivel on top of a pole. It was placed at the centre of a circle 36 metres in diameter, drawn on the ground. The marksmen chose their shooting spot on the circumference according to which direction the full outline of the parrot was facing. Prizes were awarded and, if it sounds ridiculously easy to hit a cut-out parrot from a range of 18 metres, it should be remembered that it was quite a feat with the heavy, smooth-bore muskets of those days. On occasion, members of the South African Historical Firearms Society, suitably costumed, re-enact the day's events with old-fashioned weapons.

And in the town below, the good burghers of today – and the many visitors and tourists – go about the serious and pleasurable business of tasting wines. This is a feature of a visit to any of the wine farms or co-operatives along the various wine routes (*see* maps pp93 and 94). It's also a pleasant adjunct to a tasty meal, enjoyed in a number of establishments of varying sophistication or, ideally, out of doors during the pressing season when the air is laden with the scent of grapes and an early hint of the vintage to come.

Above: *Lanzerac Hotel* (WK)
Below: *Blaauwklippen* (ER)

Co-operative wine cellars were formed partly to reduce producers' costs in various stages of wine making. Rather than every farm having its own cellars with all the necessary and expensive equipment, farmers within demarcated areas bring their crop to a central cellar belonging to the co-operative of which they are members. Wines so produced are marketed under the label of the co-operative, not of any of the subscribing farms. The first such co-operative was established in 1906, at Tulbagh, and was known as the Drostdy Cooperative. The KWV – or Ko-operatiewe Wijnbouwers Vereniging van Zuid-Afrika, Beperkt, to give its full title – was formed in 1918, and is a statutory body with various powers affecting the production of wine and spirits.

Top: *KWV* (JMc)
Middle: *Jonkershoek Valley* (ER)
Right: *Wine estate drives at Blaauwklippen* (ER)

Stellenbosch Town

Stellenbosch, despite its three centuries and its status as the second-oldest town in South Africa, conveys a spirit of youth and vigour, for this is a university town. Everywhere, students cycle, stroll, or laugh under oak trees, that have shaded many generations of inhabitants of Eikestad, or Oak Town. Perhaps the town's best-known student was the shy, serious young man who became General Jan Smuts and who met his future wife in the late 1880s, somewhere near her father's house – now Libertas Parva, an art gallery and wine museum – in Dorp Street.

Dorp Street was once the old wagon-road to Cape Town, and is one of the town's most fascinating thoroughfares, with its ancient oaks and picturesque mix of gable and cast iron, woodwork and thatch. An 'all-seeing eye of God' looks down from the gable of La Gratitude, built by a clergyman in 1798, while archways designed to admit coach and horses give tantalizing glimpses of cosy courtyards. You can eat and drink at several places in Dorp Street, and buy a variety of goods from works of art to country produce.

The Village Museum in Ryneveld Street comprises a collection of adjoining buildings, covering the life and times of urban Stellenbosch from the early years of the settlement, right through to the first quarter of this century. Little Schreuderhuis is believed to be the oldest town house in South Africa, built before 1710 and once again creating the simple ambience of the home of an ordinary burgher of those distant days. Even the small garden is planted as it probably would have been when Sebastiaan Schreuder lived here. Other houses in the complex show the life of later, wealthier citizens of a more assured village as Stellenbosch prospered.

Top: *Ida's Valley* (JS)
Middle left: *High Rustenburg Health Hydro* (ER)
Middle right: *Coetzenburg* (JS)
Right: *Dorp Street* (ER)

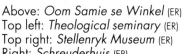

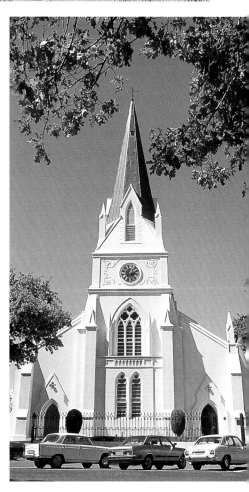

Above: *Oom Samie se Winkel* (ER)
Top left: *Theological seminary* (ER)
Top right: *Stellenryk Museum* (ER)
Right: *Schreuderhuis* (ER)
Below left: *Burgerhuis* (JS)
Far right: *De Moederkerk, Stellenbosch* (ER)

Around the village green, known as Die Braak, is a collection of gracious buildings in the old Rhenish Mission complex, and there is a thatched Coachman's Cottage where, so far as is known, no coachman ever lived. Here, too, is gabled Burgerhuis and the thatched St Mary's Church, and the distinctly curious-looking building of 1777, that once served as the official armoury, and now again houses a collection of weapons. On one end wall can be seen the letters VOC, representing the Netherlands 'Verenigde Oostindische Compagnie', founders and proprietors for almost 150 years of the Cape settlement.

Stellenbosch has many treasures tucked away in its side streets, from an ornate old gateway, to a row of model cottages designed by one of the British Empire's leading architects for no less a personality than arch-imperialist Cecil Rhodes. A stroll of exploration is well rewarded.

Paarl

When the first explorer from the Castle saw the great granite dome of Paarl Rock in the distance, the sun's early rays were dazzling on its smooth, dew-covered dome, and he wrote of the 'Diamant- en de Peerlberg' – the mountain of diamonds and pearls. The three largest granite boulders in South Africa lie here on Paarl Mountain, and they are named Bretagne, Gordon's Rock and Paarl Rock.

The town beneath the rocks grew from 1690, so is just five years younger than Stellenbosch. People speak of it as 'die Pêrel', rather than just as Paarl. In 1688, a number of Huguenot refugees from France were among the early settlers to be granted farming land here, and they started a tradition of wine-making in the green valley of the Berg River. Overlooking it all is the soaring monument to the Afrikaans language, unveiled in 1975, and a flower-lined circular mountain drive provides fine views across town and vineyard. Several vineyards and farms are actually well within the limits of the town, which has a main street about 10 kilometres long, said to be the longest main street in any country town in South Africa.

It is an interesting street, lined with many buildings that speak of different aspects and ages of the town's growth. The Strooidakkerk or 'thatched roof church' was consecrated in 1805, although a church had stood near here for many years before that. The churchyard is quaint for the number of tombs to which artisans, now long dead, added a gable, in imitation of the styles then in vogue. Down the way is the old parsonage, dating from 1786, and the home, no longer of the resident domi-nee but, as a museum, with a collection of the many domestic items indispensable to a bygone family.

Above: *Paarl Rock shining like a pearl* (ER)
Right: *Fairview goats* (ER)

Just opposite the old parsonage is the gymnasium of 1858, a year when architects and the public generally, even in distant Paarl, were fascinated by Egyptian artefacts. The pleasing result – Egyptian Revival – can be seen. Cape Revival is the style of La Concorde, headquarters of the KWV, where fascinating conducted tours may be undertaken through the biggest wine and brandy cellars in the world.

The Paarl-Wellington Wine Route takes in several estates and co-operative wineries, and offers an opportunity to taste not just the wines, but other delicacies of the district – such as waterblommetjiebredie – a meat stew made with a type of water lily. Among the other discoveries to be made are the many scenic delights, of old houses that seem to sleep in the shade of oaks and of time that has stood still.

Below: *Paarl vineyard* (ER)

Above: *Nederburg* (ER)
Right: *Strooidakkerk* (ER)

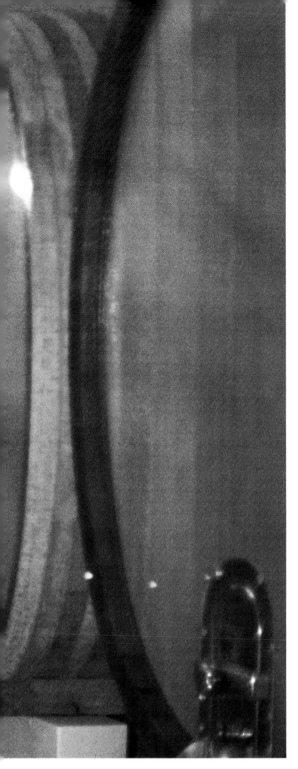

Top right: *Taalmonument* (ER)
Right: *Waterblommetjie festival* (ER)

Paarl Town

Unlike most towns and villages in the Cape, early Paarl was never really laid out according to a plan around some central building, such as a church. It just grew gradually along the wagon road that has become its Main Street. There was a church, of course, but originally it was at the place now called Simondium, after the Reverend Pierre Simond, who accompanied the French Huguenots to the Cape as their minister. In the fertile valley of Drakenstein he mixed his clerical duties with running two farms. Paarl is ringed by farms, many still set in their rolling vineyards, others now dreaming of past glories on just a small section of their former lands.

Nederburg is one of the most gracious old homesteads and an important winery that has produced an astounding number of award-winning wines. It is an appropriate venue for the annual auction of rare wines that attracts buyers from around the world, first held in 1975. Only holders of liquor licences may bid, but to receive an invitation to attend as a guest, and partake of the sumptuous luncheon, is regarded as a rare honour.

Praise for Paarl came early, and has come from distinguished pens. In 1836, a young naturalist named Charles Darwin, who was travelling around the world on the ship HMS *Beagle*, hired horses and a guide in Cape Town and rode to Paarl. He admired the winter-flowering heaths and ericas, climbed the mountain and rode slowly through the village, of which he wrote that it 'possessed an air of quiet and respectable comfort'. Twenty years later, it was described as 'about the most quaint, picturesque, peculiar and interesting town in the Cape'. The 'solitary street' was lined with oaks and pines, and the houses were 'as scrupulously clean and white as paint and lime can make them ...' These are images that are treasured by the people of Paarl, images they like to preserve.

Almost as much as Franschhoek, Paarl is the land of the Huguenots, many of whose surnames are still to be found in local directories. When these French refugees arrived it was to learn that the Dutch settlers had named the mountains Limietberge, 'the mountains at the limits'. Thinking the Dutch were referring to the mountains as the end of the world, the French light-heartedly (and unofficially) named their new home Val du Charon, a reference to

Above: *Taalmonument* (GC)
Below: *Paarl Rock* (ER)

the mythological ferryman of Hades. It seems a curious name for so beautiful a place, but it survives only in memory.

More tangible reminders of these pioneering French Protestants are their vigorous descendants, and the names they left on the countryside, like Non Pareil, Languedoc and St Omer. They are honoured by the preservation of old cemeteries, both in the Paarl district on the farm Kleinbosch at Daljosaphat, and at Franschhoek. For a good panoramic look at their countryside, you can take the helicopter ride, or drive up the Du Toit's Kloof Pass or the Jan Phillips Mountain Drive.

Above: *Wine tasting at Nederburg* (GC)
Below: *Inside the Strooidakkerk* (ER)

THE WINELANDS OF SOUTH AFRICA

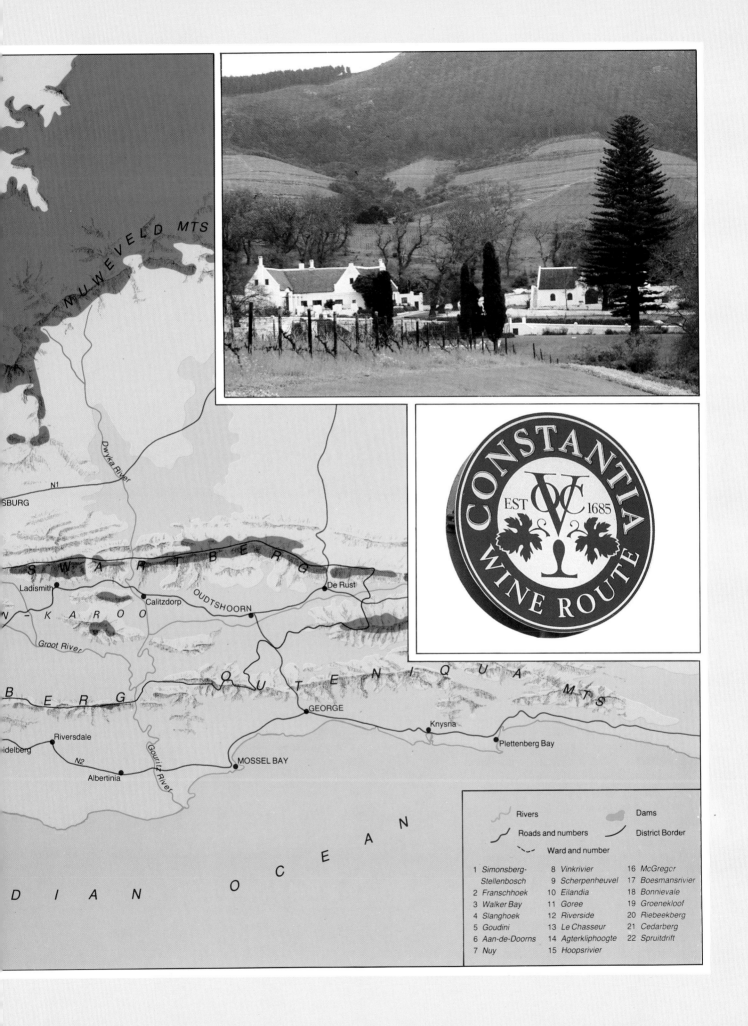

NUWEVELD MTS

Dwyka River

N1
SBURG

SWARTBERG
Ladismith
Calitzdorp
OUDTSHOORN
De Rust
N-KAROO
Groot River

BERG
OUTENIQUA MTS
GEORGE
Knysna
Plettenberg Bay

idelberg
Riversdale
N2
Albertinia
Gouritz River
MOSSEL BAY

DIAN OCEAN

CONSTANTIA
WINE ROUTE
EST 1685
VOC

Rivers
Dams
Roads and numbers
District Border
Ward and number

1 Simonsberg-
  Stellenbosch
2 Franschhoek
3 Walker Bay
4 Slanghoek
5 Goudini
6 Aan-de-Doorns
7 Nuy
8 Vinkrivier
9 Scherpenheuvel
10 Eilandia
11 Goree
12 Riverside
13 Le Chasseur
14 Agterkliphoogte
15 Hoopsrivier
16 McGregor
17 Boesmansrivier
18 Bonnievale
19 Groenekloof
20 Riebeekberg
21 Cedarberg
22 Spruitdrift

Helicopter Trip

The eagle's view is perhaps the most majestic there is. It takes in, all at once, the craggy, mountain spine of the Cape Peninsula, set in its shimmering sea that, from the heights, seems wrinkled and slowly crawling. For those whose time is short or those who want the wider view, a number of organizations operate helicopters from bases within the harbour area. A flight can be arranged according to your preference and available time, or you can sit back and follow the full, scheduled flight, with the panorama of the fairest Cape unfolding beneath you.

From the air you can relate the topography that visitors – and even locals – find so confusing. Now you can look down on the great table, sloping down to Constantia Nek, dropping steeply above the bowl of the city, and ruggedly fissured above the forests of Newlands and the garden haven of Kirstenbosch. Ribbons of roadway follow the easiest contours, a flashing stream of vehicles here, and a tree-closed, winding avenue there, along which the people of the peninsula and their guests from around the world come and go.

You can see most clearly now how the lives of Capetonians are dictated by their mountain. Behind the reclaimed land of the Foreshore and harbour, a natural amphitheatre is formed by Signal Hill, Lion's Head, Table Mountain and Devil's Peak. Each has its cluster of houses, clinging ever more precariously, it seems, as they creep higher up the slopes. Highest of all are the buildings around the upper cable station with, halfway down to the city, the ruins of the forts that, in the days of muzzle-loading cannons, were such important defence-works.

Above: *Table Mountain, Lion's Head, and Cape Town city and harbour* (MvA)
Below: *Lion's Head and Signal Hill looking towards Sea Point* (MvA)

The Cape Flats are well named, although their former sandy vastness is increasingly covered by new suburbs of Greater Cape Town, and roads and bridges radiate and double back in orderly chaos. Most of the rivers are tamed, too, and make their regulated way to the sea through concrete canals, but an expanse of wetlands on the Liesbeeck is still the haunt of wheeling seabirds, small scatterings of white far below the airborne traveller. There are the lakes, too; Rondevlei, a bird sanctuary which once again is home to a hippopotamus family, and Princess Vlei, the lake formed by the tears of a Khoikhoi princess, as she was carried away captive by early navigators.

Far removed from the perils of the sea you can look down on its handiwork of rock and wreck, peering through its crystal depths to the seabed on days that are very still. From above False Bay watch the steady, majestic march of the incoming rollers eagerly awaited by the little dots that are surf enthusiasts, and the bright sails that shimmer like insects' wings on the waters of nearby Sandvlei. Like slow, segmented worms, trains crawl along their ordained pathways by the seaside, through sprawls of house and factory and out into the open between fields of grape and wheat, orchard and grassland.

To the west, the great Atlantic rolls in to shores that are white beach and grey-brown rock, with here and there a small boat riding the swells as patient men reap their harvest of the sea. And as Cape Town falls ever further behind, you come to the curve of mountains that the settlers called 'the mountains of Africa', mountains that seriously restricted their advance to the interior, now crossed – so simply, it seems – by streamers of asphalt highway. Here, the rivers run free, and the Berg River winds its own way through the grateful lands that draw from it much of their sustenance.

Above: *Fish Hoek valley with Hout Bay in the background* (MvA)
Below: *Robben Island* (MvA)

You may come gently to earth on green lawns, that once knew the measured tread of sturdy horses that pulled their cartloads of grapes to the cellars where, in time-honoured fashion, the juice was pressed by the bare feet of slaves, moving to a different tempo. How far away it all seems in time, but somehow still close and attainable, in a beautiful corner of the world where much has changed, but that which is best remains.

Above: *Hout Bay from Cape Hangklip* (MvA)
Top left: *Bantry Bay and Sea Point* (JM)
Left: *View to Kommetjie from above Table Mountain* (GC)
Below: *University of Cape Town* (GC)

Above: *Cape Flats* (MvA)
Below: *Sea Point backed by Table Mountain and Signal Hill* (MvA)

CAPE TOWN CENTRAL   KAAPSTAD SENTRAAL

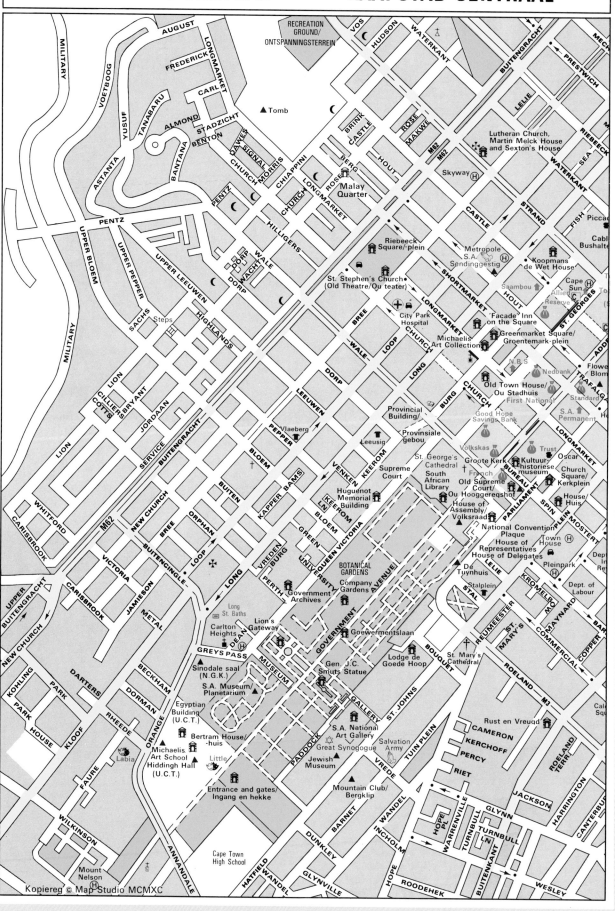

RECREATION GROUND/ONTSPANNINGSTERREIN

▲ Tomb

Malay Quarter

Lutheran Church, Martin Melck House and Sexton's House

Skyway Ⓗ

Piccadi

Cabl
Bushalte

Riebeeck Square/-plein

Metropole
S.A. Sendinggestig

Koopmans
de Wet House

Cape
Sun Ⓗ

Saambou

St. Stephen's Church
(Old Theatre/Ou teater)

City Park Hospital

'Facade' Inn
on the Square

Allied
Reserve

Greenmarket Square/
Groentemark-plein

Michaelis
Art Collection

N.B.S

Flowe
Blom

Nedbank

Old Town House/
Ou Stadhuis

First National

Standard

Provincial
Building/
Provinsiale
gebou

Good Hope
Savings Bank

S.A.
Permanent

Vlaeberg

Leeusig

Volkskas

Trust

Oscar

Kultuur-
historiese
museum

St. George's
Cathedral

South
African
Library

Groote Kerk

French

Old Supreme
Court/
Ou Hooggeregshof

Church
Square/
Kerkplein

House/
Huis

Supreme
Court

Huguenot
Memorial
Building

BUREAU

House
of Assembly/
Volksraad

National Convention
Plaque
House of
Representatives
House of Delegates

Town
House Ⓗ

De
Tuynhuis

Pleinpark

Dept
In
Re

BOTANICAL
GARDENS

Company
Gardens

Stalplein

Dept. of
Labour

Government
Archives

Goewermentslaan

Lodge de
Goede Hoop

St. Mary's
Cathedral

Long
St. Baths Ⓗ

Carlton
Heights

Lion's
Gateway

GREYS PASS

Gen. J.C.
Smuts Statue

Rust en Vreuqd

CAMERON

Sinodale saal
(N.G.K.)

S.A. Museum/
Planetarium

S.A. National
Art Gallery

Egyptian
Building
(U.C.T.)

Bertram House/
-huis

Great Synagogue

Salvation
Army

KERCHOFF

PERCY

Michaelis
Art School
Hiddingh Hall
(U.C.T.)

Labia

Little

Jewish
Museum

RIET

Entrance and gates/
Ingang en hekke

Mountain Club/
Bergklip

Mount
Nelson

Cape Town
High School

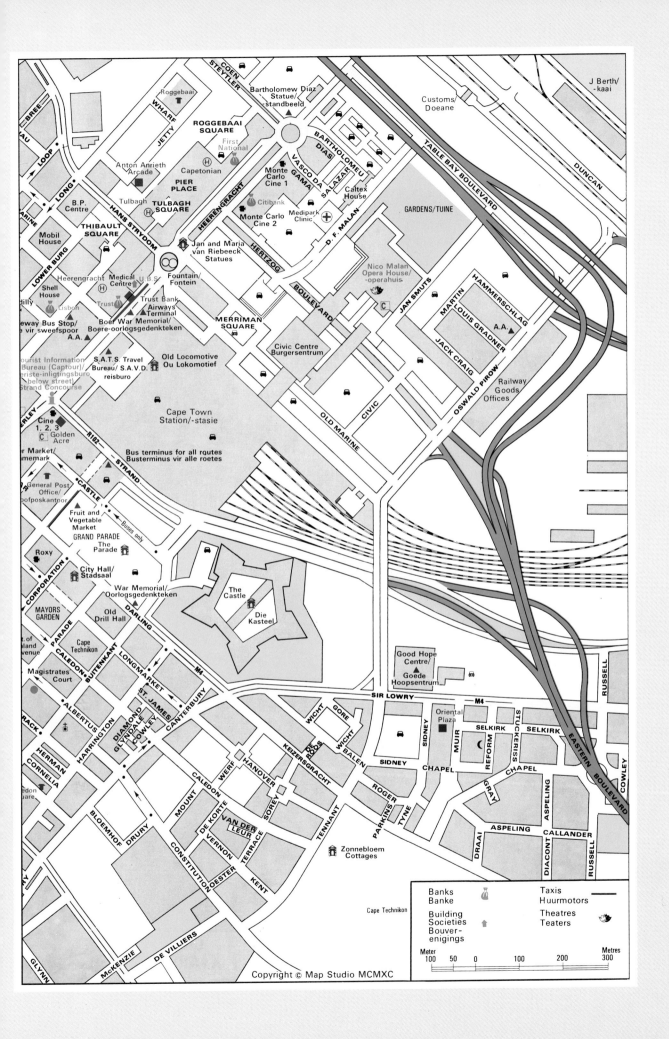

Copyright © Map Studio MCMXC

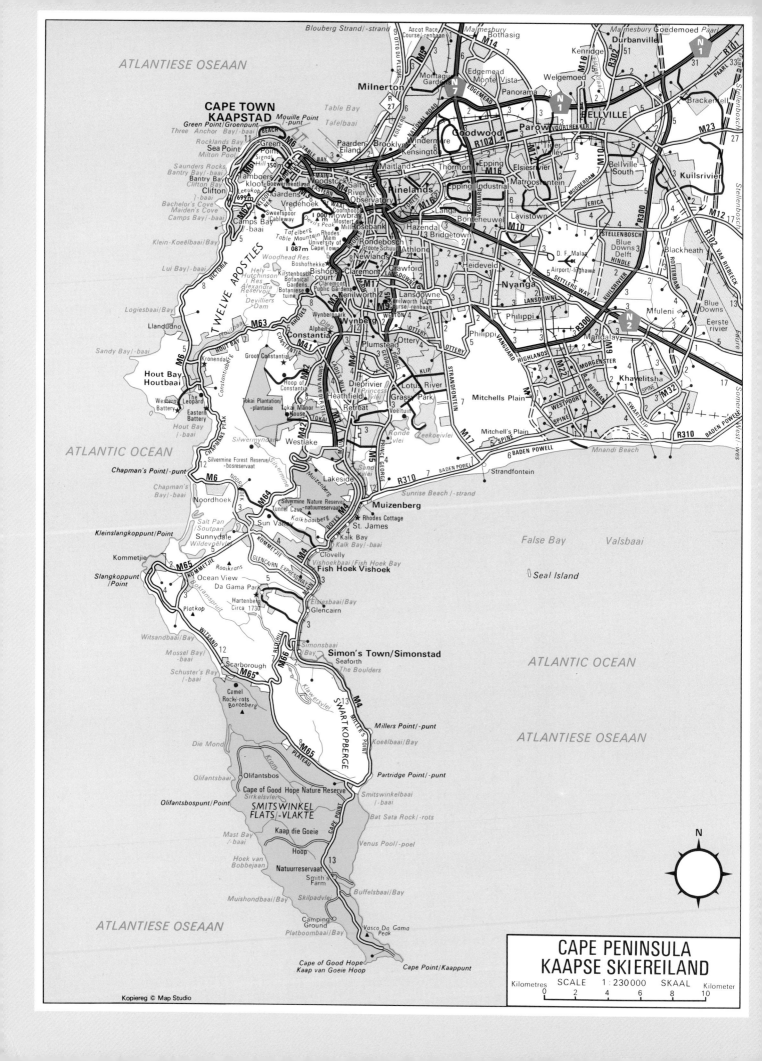

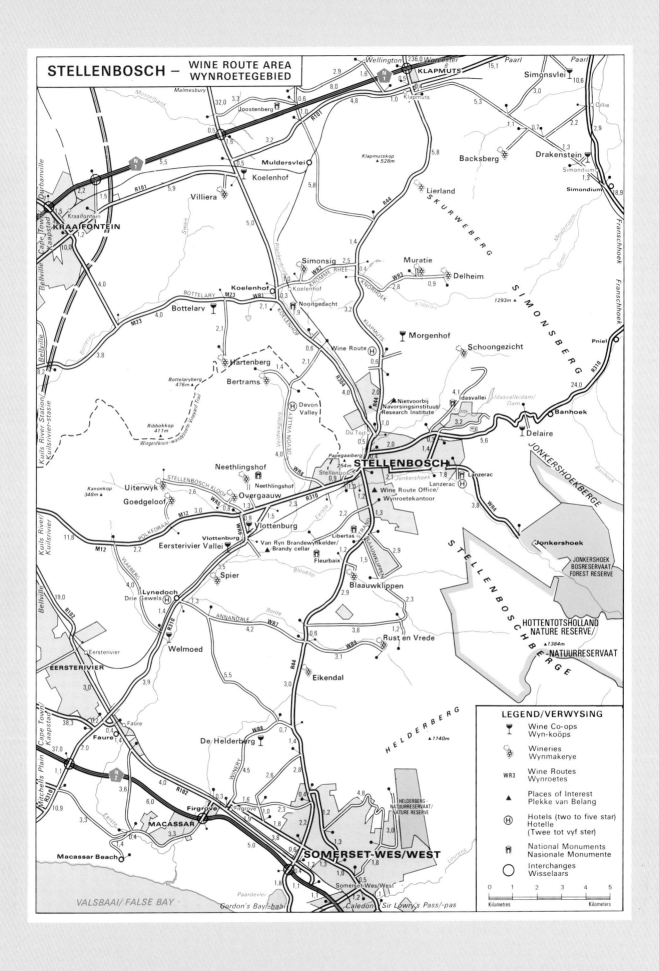

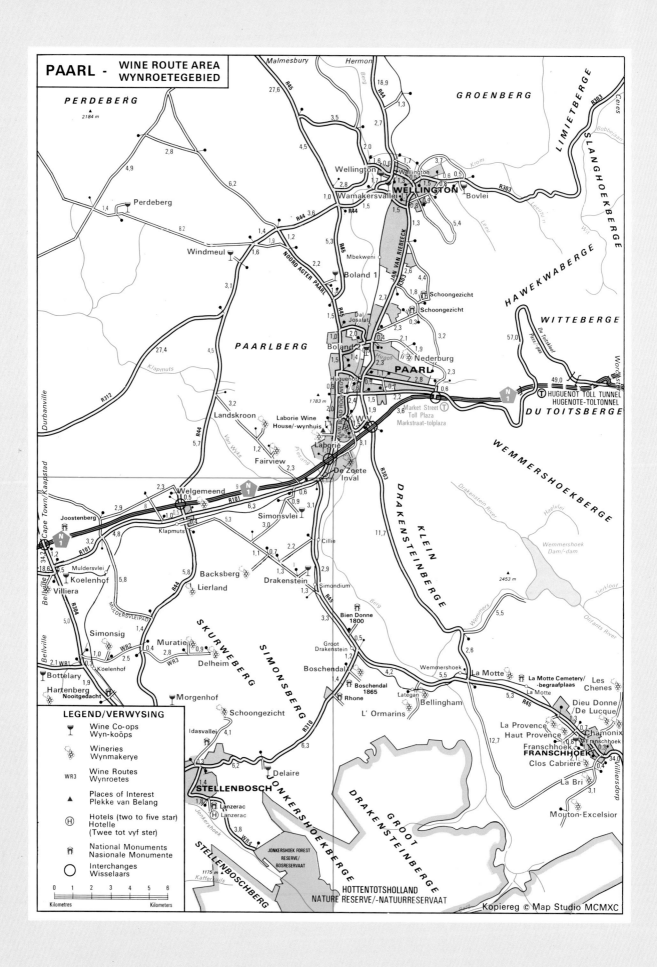

Index